Arabic—English

Bilingual Visual
Dictionary

Milet

Milet Publishing
Smallfields Cottage, Cox Green
Rudgwick, Horsham, West Sussex
RH12 3DE England
info@milet.com
www.milet.com
www.milet.co.uk

First English-Arabic edition published by Milet Publishing in 2012

ISBN 978 1 84059 684 7

Designed by Christangelos Seferiadis

Printed and bound in Turkey by Ertem Matbaası

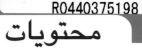

Contents محتويات

■ **Animals**
Birds...4
Domestic Animals...7
Insects...10
Reptiles & Amphibians...12
Sea Creatures...14
Wild Animals...16

■ **The Human Body**...*21*

■ **House**
Structure of House...24
Living Room...25
Bedroom...26
Bathroom...27
Dining Room...28
Kitchen...29
Household Objects...32
Domestic Appliances...34

■ **Clothing & Personal objects**
Clothing...38
Personal Objects...42

■ **Tools**...*48*

■ **Technology**...*52*

■ **Food**...*54*
Fruit & Vegetables...55
Bakery...62
Nuts...64
Meat...65
Miscellaneous Food...66
Dairy Products...70
Beverages...71

■ **Transportation**
Vehicles...72
Other...80

■ **Nature**
Plants...82
Land Forms...89
Weather...94

■ **Earth and Space**
Earth...96
Space...98
Environment...100

■ **Sports**...*102*

■ **The Arts**...*108*

■ **Musical Instruments**...*110*

■ **Time**...*114*

■ **School**...*118*

■ **Numbers**...*124*

■ **Shapes & Colors**
Shapes...130
Colors...132

■ **Punctuation Marks**...*134*

■ **Symbols**...*135*

■ **Index**...*136*

حيوانات
طيور.....................4
حيوانات منزلية.....................7
حشرات.....................10
الزواحف والبرمائيات.....12
حيوانات بحرية.....................14
حيوانات برية.....................16

جسم الإنسان.....................21

بيت
بنية البيت.....................24
غرفة الجلوس.....................25
غرفة نوم.....................26
حمام.....................27
غرفة الطعام.....................28
مطبخ.....................29
معدات منزلية.....................32
أجهزة منزلية.....................34

ملابس وأشياء شخصية
ملابس.....................38
أشياء شخصية.....................42

أدوات.....................48

تكنلوجيا.....................52

طعام.....................54
فواكه وخضروات.....................55
مخبز.....................62
مكسرات.....................64
لحم.....................65
أنواع متفرقة من الطعام.............66
منتجات من مشتقات الألبان.....70
مشروبات.....................71

وسائل النقل
السيارات.....................72
أخرى.....................80

الطبيعة
نباتات.....................82
تضاريس.....................89
الطقس.....................94

الأرض والفضاء
كوكب الأرض.....................96
الفضاء.....................98
البيئة.....................100

رياضات.....................102

فنون.....................108

آلات موسيقية.....................110

الوقت.....................114

مدرسة.....................118

الأرقام.....................124

أشكال وألوان
أشكال.....................130
ألوان.....................132

علامات الترقيم.....134

إشارات.....................135

مؤشر.....................136

robin
طائر أبو الحن

crow
غراب

cage
قفص

beak
منقار

eagle
نسر

claw
مخلب

feather
ريشة

egg
بيضة

falcon
صقر

flamingo
طائر البشروس

gull
نورس

hawk
صقر

heron
مالك الحزين

lovebird
طيور الحب

nest
عش

ostrich
نعامة

owl
بومة

parrot
ببغاء

peacock
طاووس

5

pelican

طائر البجع

pigeon

حمامة

sparrow

عصفور الدوري

stork

اللقلق

swallow

طائر السنونو

swan

بجعة

vulture

نسر

wing

جناح الطائر

woodpecker

نقار الخشب

barn
إسطبل

bull
ثور

calf
عجل

cow
بقرة

cat
قطة

kitten
هرة صغيرة

dog
كلب

doghouse
بيت الكلب

puppy
جرو

collar
طوق

chick
صوص

crest
عرف الديك

goose
إوزة

hen
دجاجة

rooster
ديك

duck
بطة

turkey
ديك حبش

lamb

خروف

goat

ماعز

sheep

غنم

camel

جمل

pig

خنزير

donkey

حمار

pet

حيوان أليف

horse

حصان

hoof

....

حافر الفرس

ant
نملة

moth
عُثّة

beetle
خنفساء

cocoon
شرنقة

caterpillar
يرقانة الفراشة

butterfly
فراشة

cricket
الجدجد

grasshopper
جُندب

dragonfly
يَعسوب

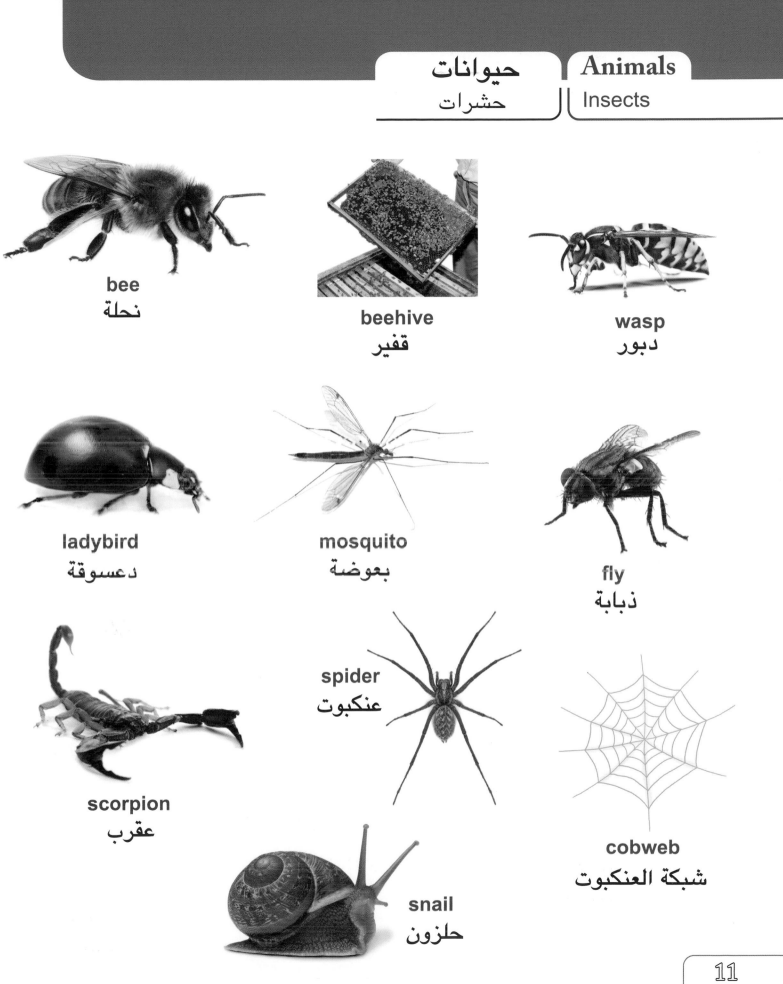

bee
نحلة

beehive
قفير

wasp
دبور

ladybird
دعسوقة

mosquito
بعوضة

fly
ذبابة

scorpion
عقرب

spider
عنكبوت

cobweb
شبكة العنكبوت

snail
حلزون

chameleon
حرباء

frog
ضفدع

crocodile
تمساح

iguana
إيغوانا

newt
سمندل الماء

lizard
سحلية

earthworm
دودة الأرض

salamander
السمندر

snake
أفعة

tadpole
شرغوف

tortoise
سلحفاة

toad
ضفدع

crab
سرطان

jellyfish
قنديل البحر

crayfish
جراد البحر

dolphin
دلفين

lobster
سرطان البحر

whale
حوت

fish
سمكة

octopus
أخطبوط

seahorse
فرس البحر

penguin
البطريق

seal
فقمة

shark
سمك القرش

walrus
حصان البحر

starfish
نجم البحر

turtle
سلحفاة

seaweed
عشب البحر

coral
مرجان

bat
خفّاش

bear
دب

koala
الكوال

polar bear
دب قطبي

elephant
فيل

tusk
ناب

raccoon
حيوان الراكون

chimpanzee
الشمبانزي

skunk
حيوان الظربان

gorilla
غوريلا

giraffe
زرافة

fox
ثعلب

wolf
ذئب

monkey
قرد

cub
جرو الثعلب

mane
العُرف

leopard
فهد

lion
أسد

tiger
نمر

llama
حيوان اللاما

kangaroo
الكَنغَر

zebra
حمار الوحش

horn
قرن

deer
الأيل

hippopotamus
فرس النهر

fawn
الخِشف ولد الظبي

panda
الباندا

rhinoceros
وحيد القرن

mole
خلد

hedgehog
قنفذ

squirrel
سنجاب

tail
ذيل

mouse
فأر

rat
جرذ

rabbit
أرنب

otter
قُضاعة / كلب الماء

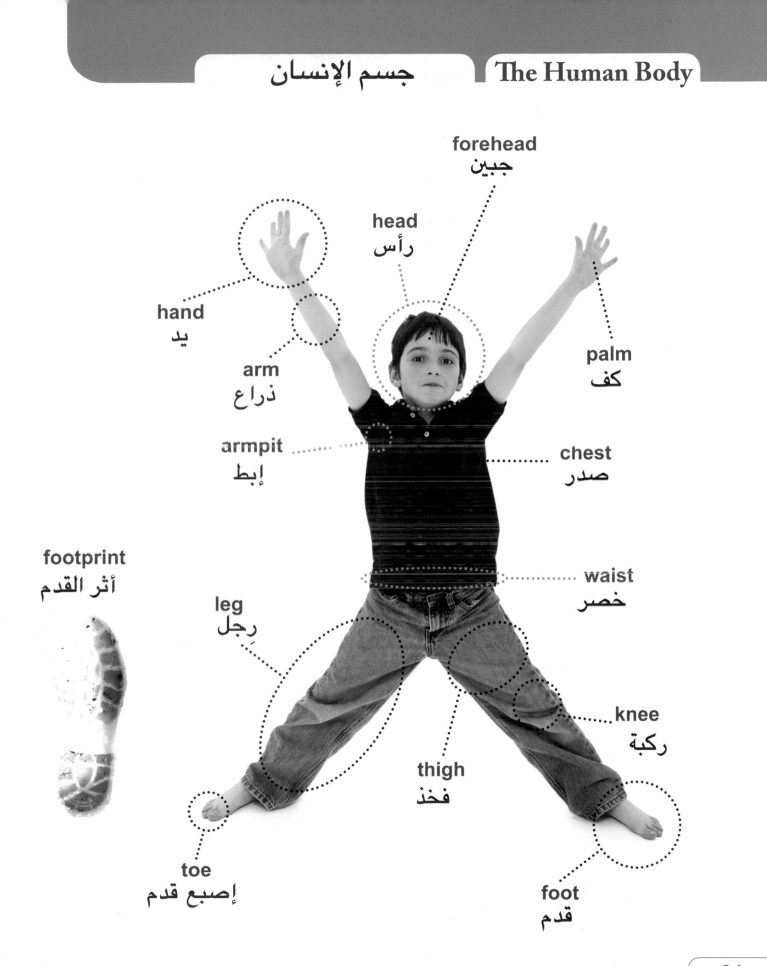

forehead
جبين

head
رأس

hand
يد

arm
ذراع

armpit
إبط

palm
كف

chest
صدر

footprint
أثر القدم

waist
خصر

leg
رِجل

knee
ركبة

thigh
فخذ

toe
إصبع قدم

foot
قدم

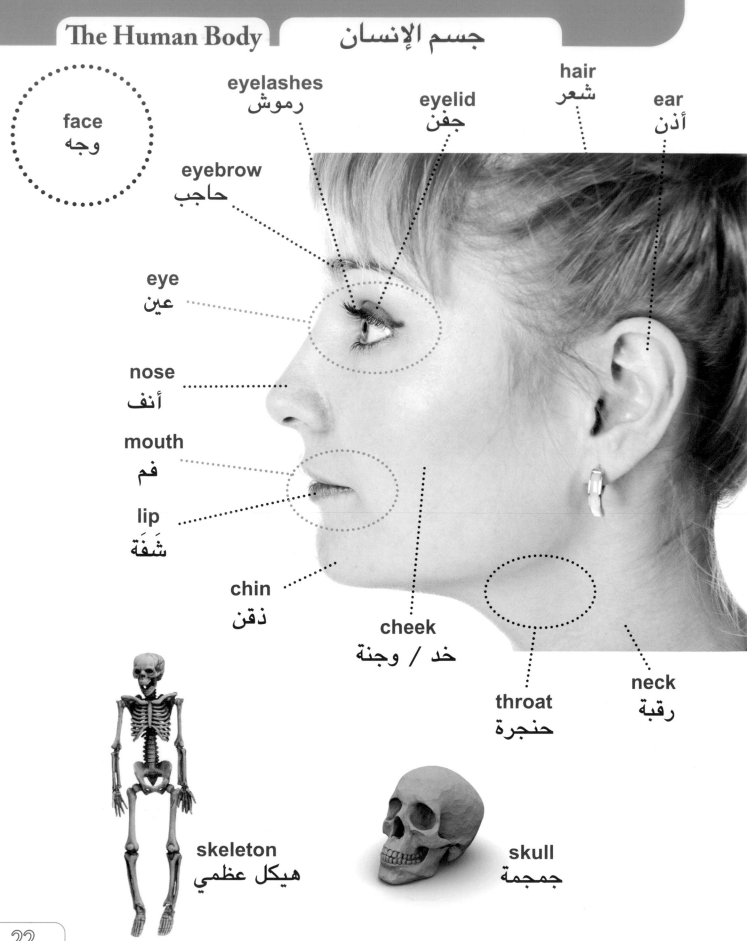

eyelashes
رموش

eyelid
جفن

hair
شعر

ear
أذن

face
وجه

eyebrow
حاجب

eye
عين

nose
أنف

mouth
فم

lip
شَفَة

chin
ذقن

cheek
خد / وجنة

throat
حنجرة

neck
رقبة

skeleton
هيكل عظمي

skull
جمجمة

shoulder
كتف

elbow
مرفق

navel
السُّرة

hip
وَرِك

shin
قصبة الرجل

calf
بطة الساق / ربلة الساق

ankle
كاحل

heel
كعب

middle finger
الإصبع الوسطى

ring finger
إصبع البنصر

index finger
السبابة

little finger
خنصر

thumb
إبهام اليد

fingerprint
بصمة

wrist
معصم

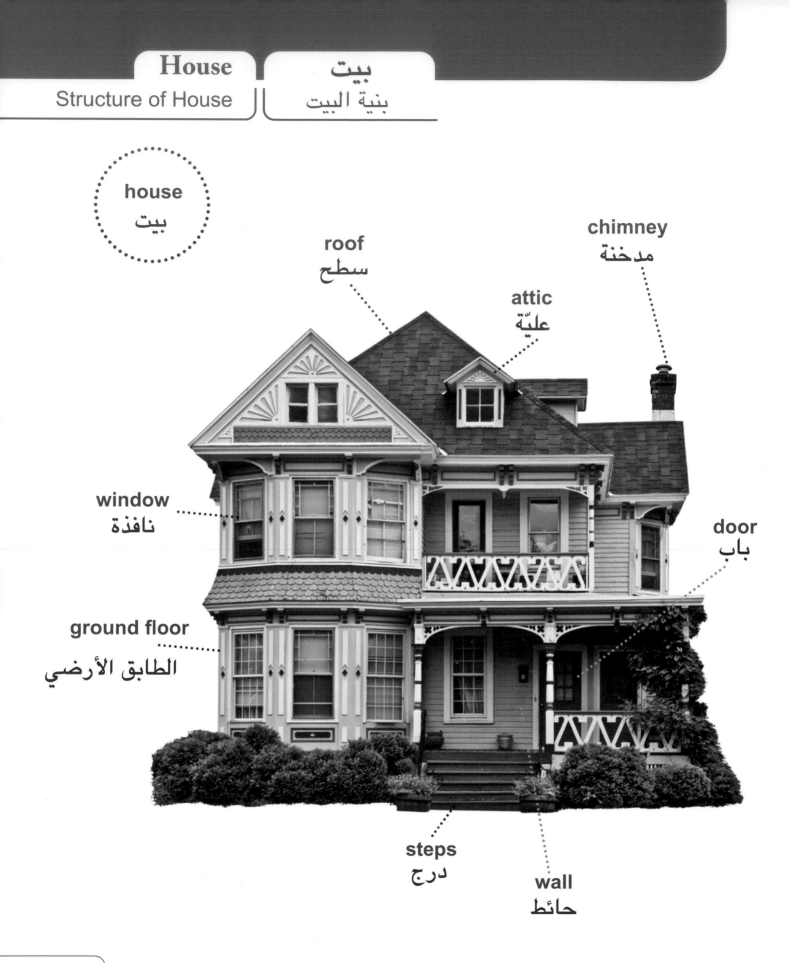

house
بيت

roof
سطح

chimney
مدخنة

attic
عليّة

window
نافذة

door
باب

ground floor
الطابق الأرضي

steps
درج

wall
حائط

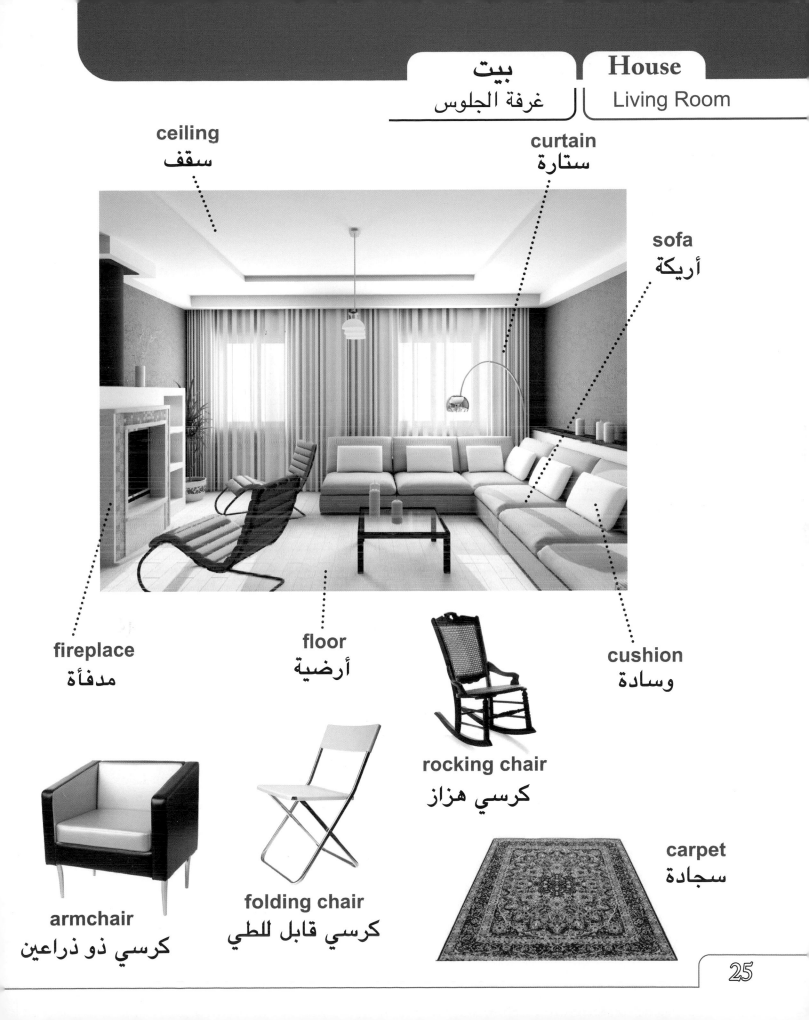

ceiling
سقف

curtain
ستارة

sofa
أريكة

fireplace
مدفأة

floor
أرضية

cushion
وسادة

rocking chair
كرسي هزاز

armchair
كرسي ذو ذراعين

folding chair
كرسي قابل للطي

carpet
سجادة

pillow
وسادة

sheet
جوخ

blanket
بطّانية

bed
سرير

wardrobe
خزانة الثياب

comforter
لحاف

rug
بساط

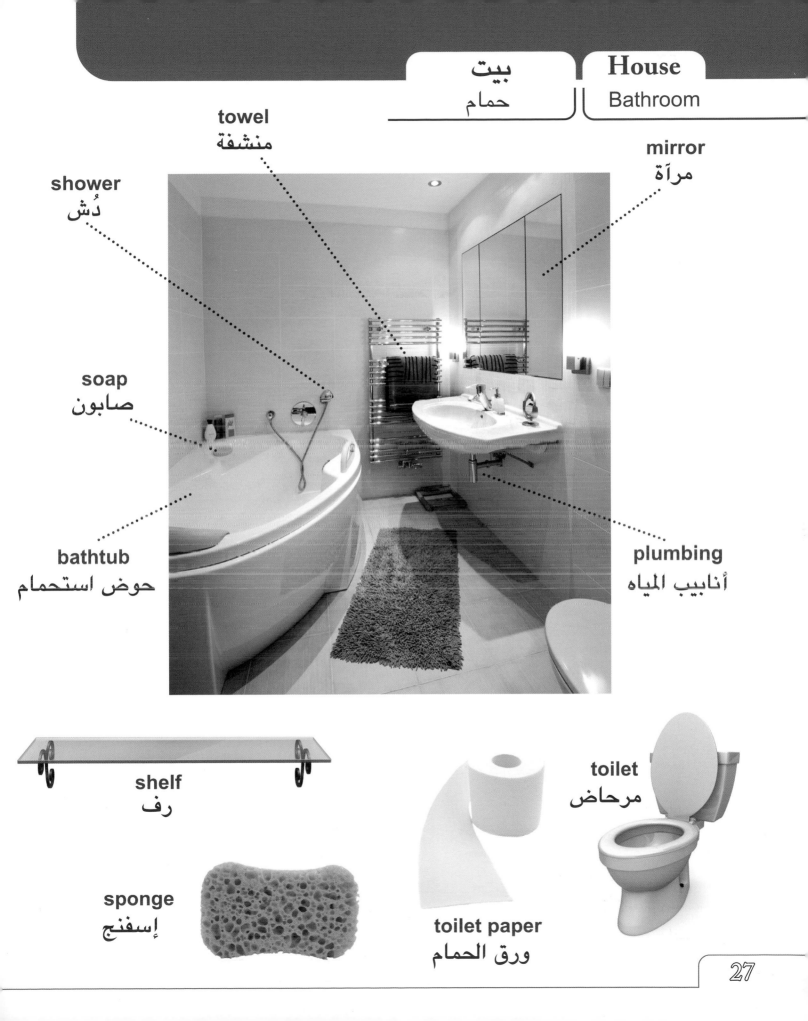

towel
منشفة

mirror
مرآة

shower
دُش

soap
صابون

bathtub
حوض استحمام

plumbing
أنابيب المياه

shelf
رف

sponge
إسفنج

toilet paper
ورق الحمام

toilet
مرحاض

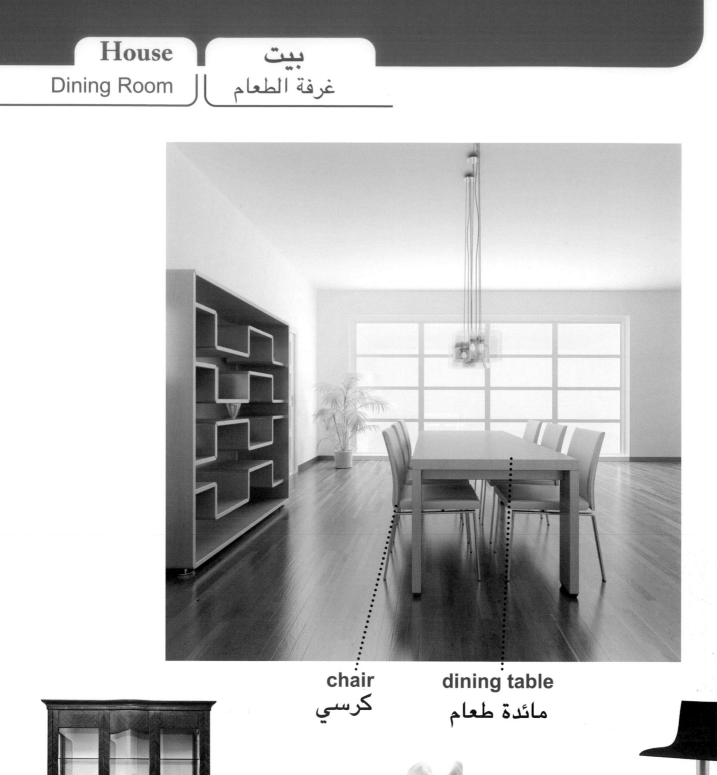

chair
كرسي

dining table
مائدة طعام

cabinet
خزانة

tableware
أدوات المائدة

stool
مقعد

refrigerator
ثلاجة

pot
إناء

bowl
زبدية

pressure cooker
قدر الضغط

frying pan
مقلاة

bottle
زجاجة

glass
كأس

jar
جرّة

shaker
مِذرّة

knife
سكّين

jug
إبريق

plate
طبق

fork
شوكة

spoon
ملعقة

scale
ميزان

sink
حوض

faucet
صنبور

cutting board
لوح لتقطيع الطعام

juice extractor
عصّارة فواكه

burner
موقد

teapot
إبريق الشاي

teaspoon
ملعقة شاي

basket
سلة

box
صندوق

broom
مكنسة

bucket
دلو

candle
شمعة

clock
ساعة حائط

clothespin
ملقط غسيل

doormat
مِمسحة الأرجل

ironing board
طاولة الكي

jerrycan
وعاء لحمل الوقود

flowerpot
إناء زهور

mop
مِمسحة

sack
كيس

vase
مزهرية

air conditioner
مكيف هواء

radiator
جهاز تدفئة جداري

ceiling fan
مروحة سقف

bedside lamp
مصباح جانب السرير

desk lamp
مصباح المكتب

chandelier
ثريّا

floor lamp
مصباح الأرضية

lamp
مصباح

toaster
آلة تحميص الخبز

deep fryer
مقلاة عميقة

electric cooker
موقد كهربائي

oven
فرن

microwave oven
المايكرويف

sewing machine
ماكينة خياطة

doorbell
جرس الباب

food processor
آلة لإعداد الطعام

electrical outlet
مأخذ التيار الكهربائي

blender
خلاط

door handle
مقبض الباب

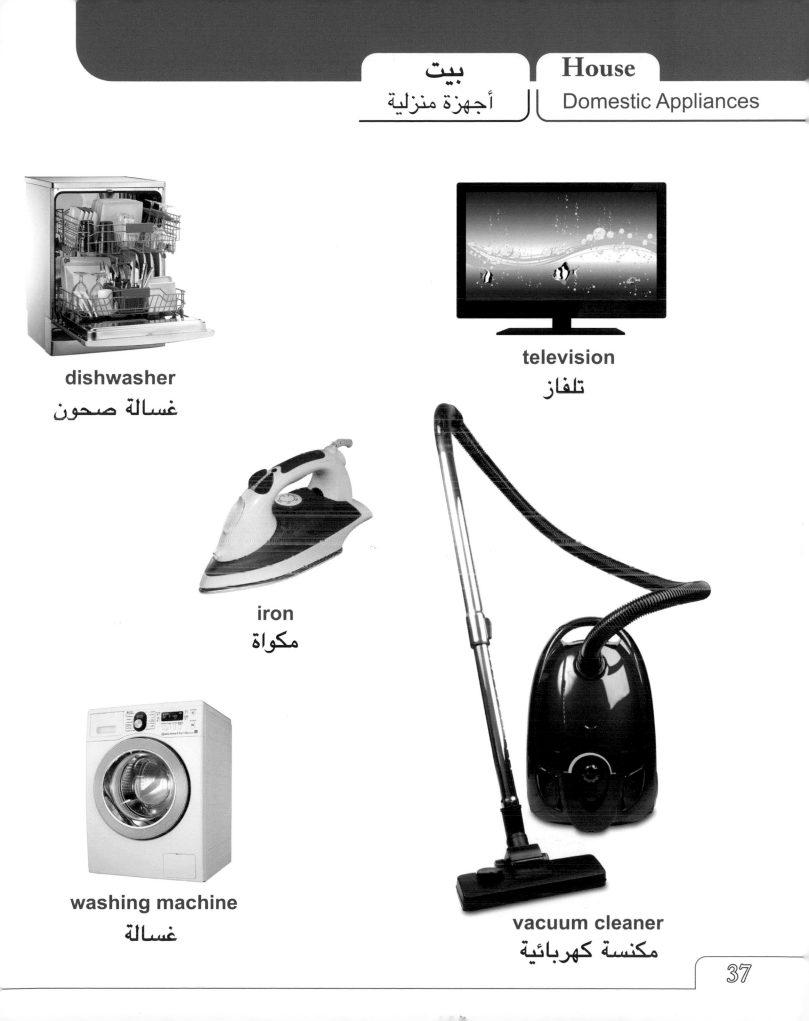

dishwasher

غسالة صحون

television

تلفاز

iron

مكواة

washing machine

غسالة

vacuum cleaner

مكنسة كهربائية

tracksuit
بدلة رياضية

suit
بدلة

dress
فستان

pocket
جيب

jumpsuit
بذلة

bathrobe
برنس حمام

swimming trunks
سروال السباحة

swimsuit
ثوب السباحة

ملابس

blouse
بُلوزة

cardigan
سترة من الصوف المحبوك

sweater
سترة

shirt
قميص

t-shirt
قميص قصير الكمّين

jeans
سروال الجينز

shorts
سروال قصير

skirt
تنورة

trousers
بنطال

cap
قبعة

beret
البيريه / قبعة مستديرة

hat
قبعة

bow tie
عقدة عنق أنشوطية

belt
حزام

tie
ربطة عنق

scarf
وشاح

foulard
وشاح حريري

glove
قفاز

ملابس وأشياء شخصية

ملابس

flip-flops
شبشب

slippers
خف

sandal
صندل

boots
حذاء طويل الرقبة / جزمة

heel
كعب الحذاء

sneakers
أحذية رياضية

shoes
حذاء

socks
جوارب

shoelaces
رباط الحذاء

emerald
زمرد

diamond
الماس

ruby
ياقوت

earrings
قرط

ring
خاتم

necklace
عِقد

bracelet
سوار

jewellery
مجوهرات

watch
ساعة يد

ملابس وأشياء شخصية
أشياء شخصية

briefcase
حقيبة جلدية

badge
شارة انتساب

backpack
حقيبة ظهر

passport
جواز سفر

shoulder bag
حقيبة كتف

suitcase
حقيبة سفر

walking stick
عصا المشي

wallet
محفظة

purse
محفظة

umbrella
مظلة

clothes brush
فرشاة الملابس

clothes hanger
شماعة ملابس

button
زر

cloth
قطعة قماش / خرقة

ribbon
شريط

reel
بكرة خيطان

thread
خيط

zipper
سحّاب

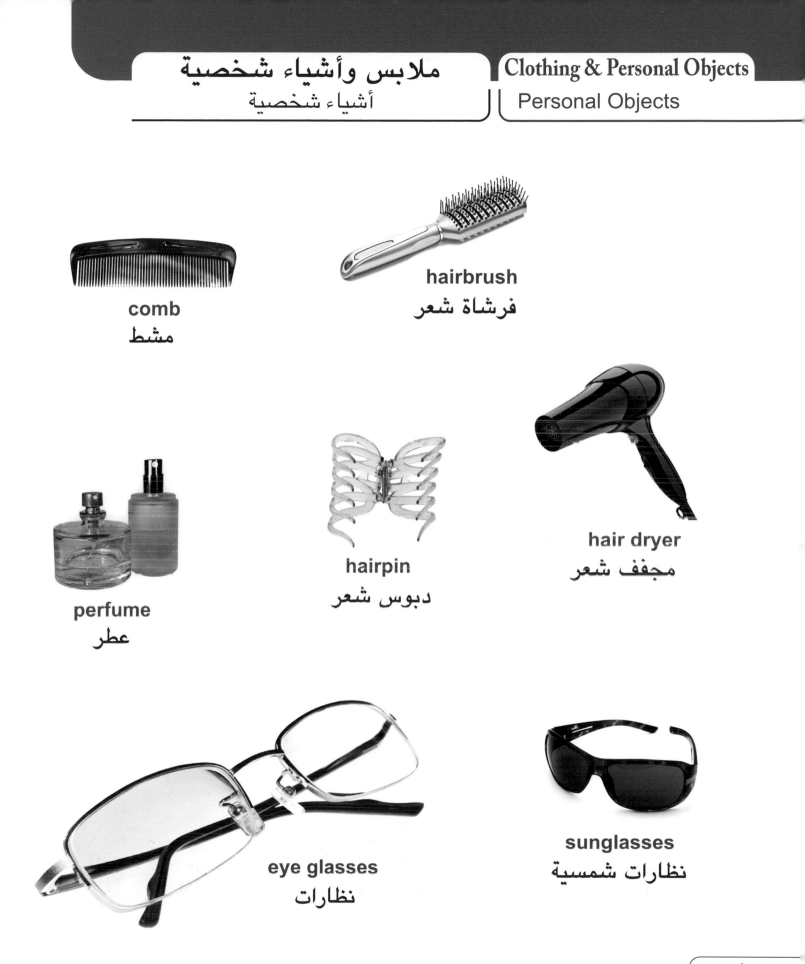

comb
مشط

hairbrush
فرشاة شعر

perfume
عطر

hairpin
دبوس شعر

hair dryer
مجفف شعر

eye glasses
نظارات

sunglasses
نظارات شمسية

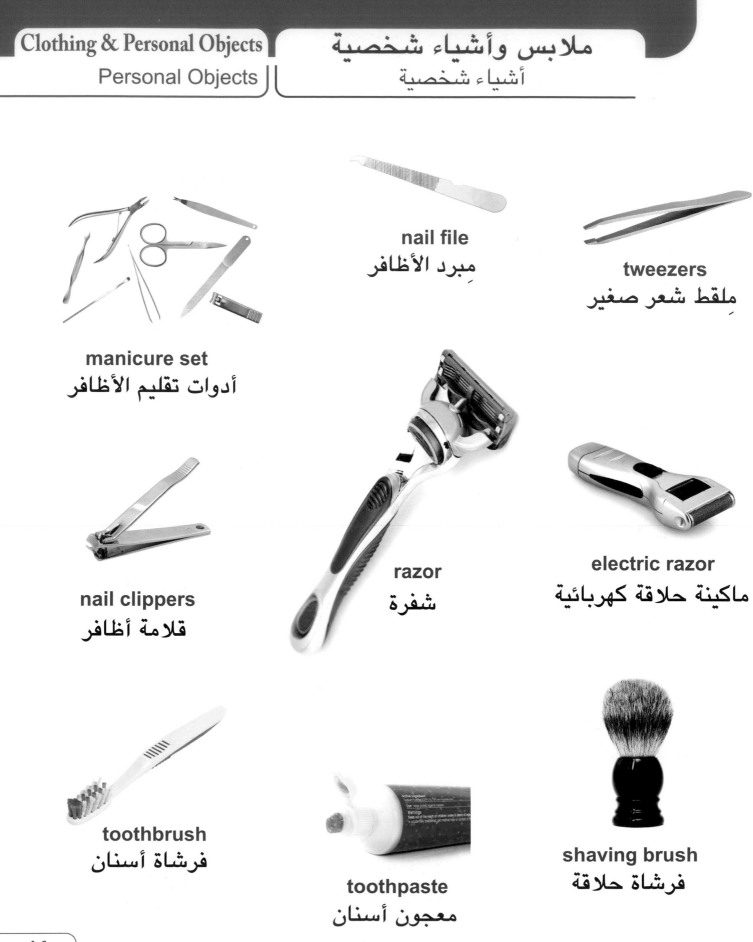

nail file
مِبرد الأظافر

tweezers
مِلقط شعر صغير

manicure set
أدوات تقليم الأظافر

razor
شفرة

electric razor
ماكينة حلاقة كهربائية

nail clippers
قلامة أظافر

toothbrush
فرشاة أسنان

toothpaste
معجون أسنان

shaving brush
فرشاة حلاقة

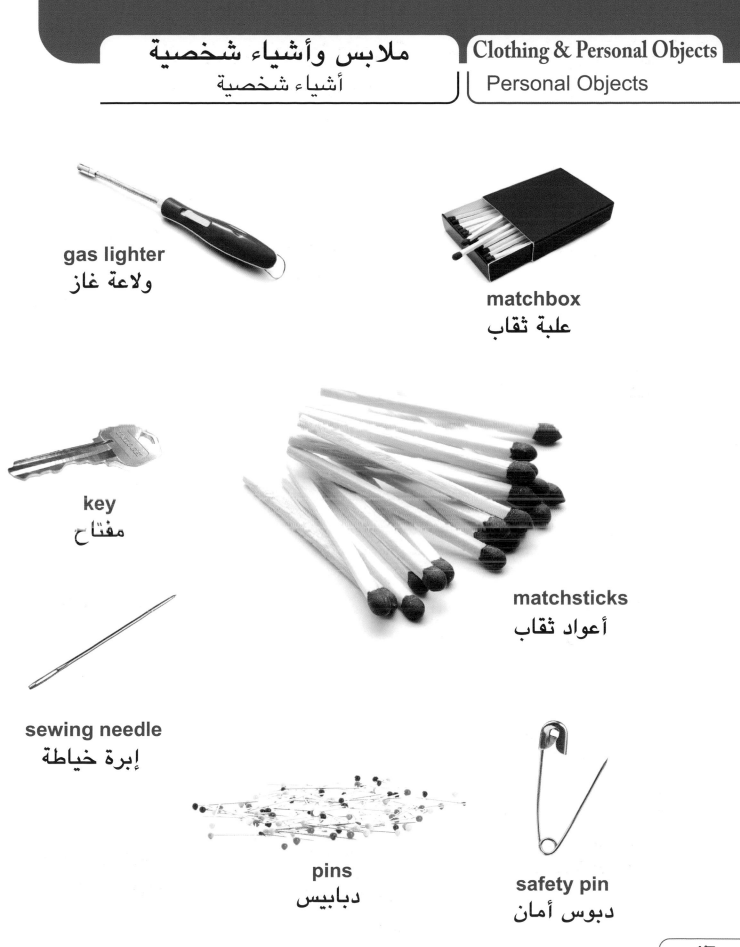

gas lighter
ولاعة غاز

matchbox
علبة ثقاب

key
مفتّاح

matchsticks
أعواد ثقاب

sewing needle
إبرة خياطة

pins
دبابيس

safety pin
دبوس أمان

adjustable wrench
مفتاح ربط قابل للتعديل

combination wrenches
مفتاح براغي

long-nose pliers
كماشة طويلة الأنف

mole wrench
مفتاح ربط

open ended wrench
مفتاح ذو نهايات مفتوحة

slip joint pliers
كماشة ذو مفصل متحرّك

nut
حزقة

toolbox
علبة أدوات

spirit level
ميزان تسوية

battery
بطارية

car battery
بطارية السيارة

drill bit
جزء المِثقب اللولبي

screw
برغي

electric drill
مثقب كهربائي

screwdriver
مفك البراغي

hammer
مطرقة

nail
مسمار

mallet
مطرقة خشبية

chain
سلسلة

fire extinguisher
مطفئة حريق

safety helmet
خوذة

padlock
ققل

ladder
سلّم

plug
قابس كهرباء

torch
مصباح يدوي

tape measure
شريط القياس

axe
فأس

chisel
إزميل

handsaw
منشار يدوي

hose
خرطوم مياه

rope
حبل

rake
مِجرف

pickax
معول

shovel
مجرفة

wheelbarrow
عربة يدوية

answering machine
جهاز استقبال المكالمات الهاتفية

telephone
هاتف

monitor
شاشة كومبيوتر

chip
رقاقة إلكترونية

computer
كومبيوتر

keyboard
لوحة المفاتيح

scanner
جهاز الماسح الضوئي

printer
طابعة

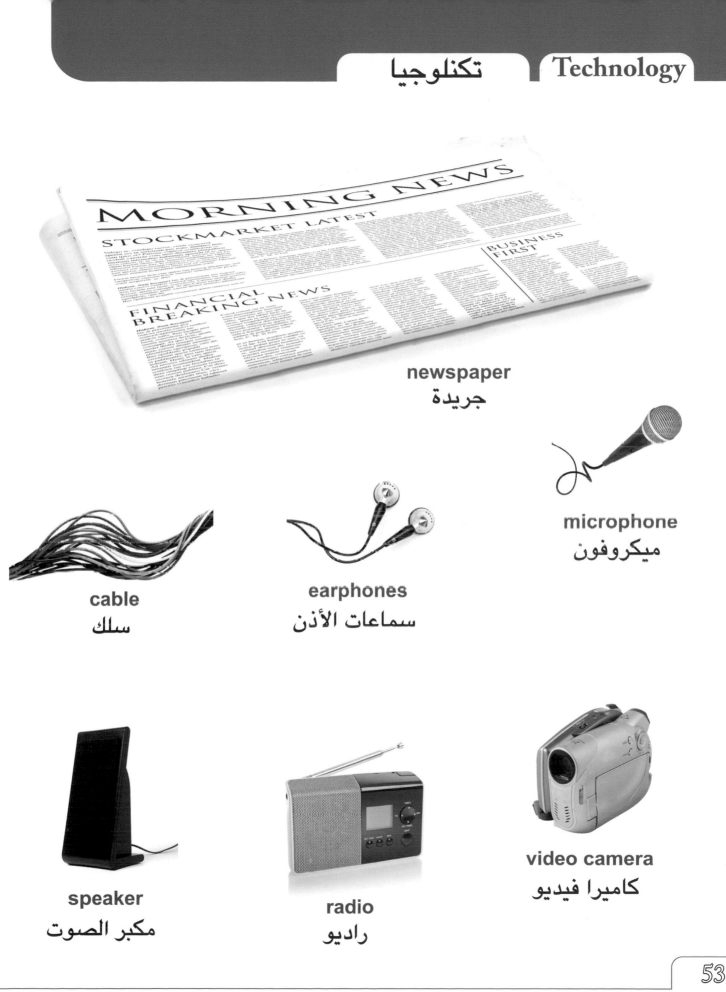

newspaper
جريدة

microphone
ميكروفون

cable
سلك

earphones
سماعات الأذن

speaker
مكبر الصوت

radio
راديو

video camera
كاميرا فيديو

supermarket
سوبر ماركت

checkout
دفع الحساب والمغادرة

market
سوق

restaurant
مطعم

appricot
مشمش

avocado
أفوكادو

apple
تفاح

blackberry
ثمر العلّيق

blueberry
ثمر العنبيّة

banana
موز

raspberry
توت

strawberry
فراولة

cherry
كرز

grape
عنب

kiwi
كيوي

peach
درّاق

grapefruit
الكريفون

mandarin
ثمر اليوسفي

orange
برتقال

melon
شمّام

watermelon
بطيخ

pear
إجاص / كمّثرى

plum
خوخ

mango
المانجو

pomegranate
رمّان

quince
سفرجل

pineapple
أناناس

coconut
جوز الهند

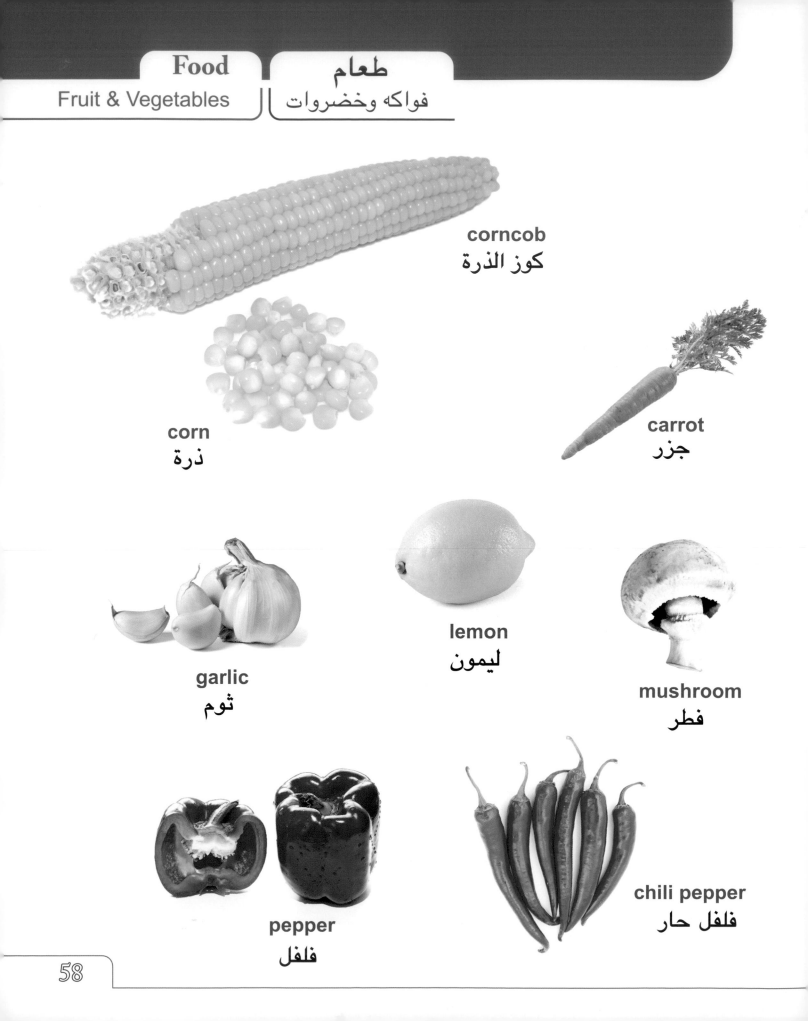

corncob
كوز الذرة

corn
ذرة

carrot
جزر

garlic
ثوم

lemon
ليمون

mushroom
فطر

pepper
فلفل

chili pepper
فلفل حار

cucumber
خيار

tomato
طماطم

onion
بصل

potato
بطاطا

pumpkin
قرع / يقطين

okra
بامية

green bean
فاصوليا خضراء

peas
بازلاء

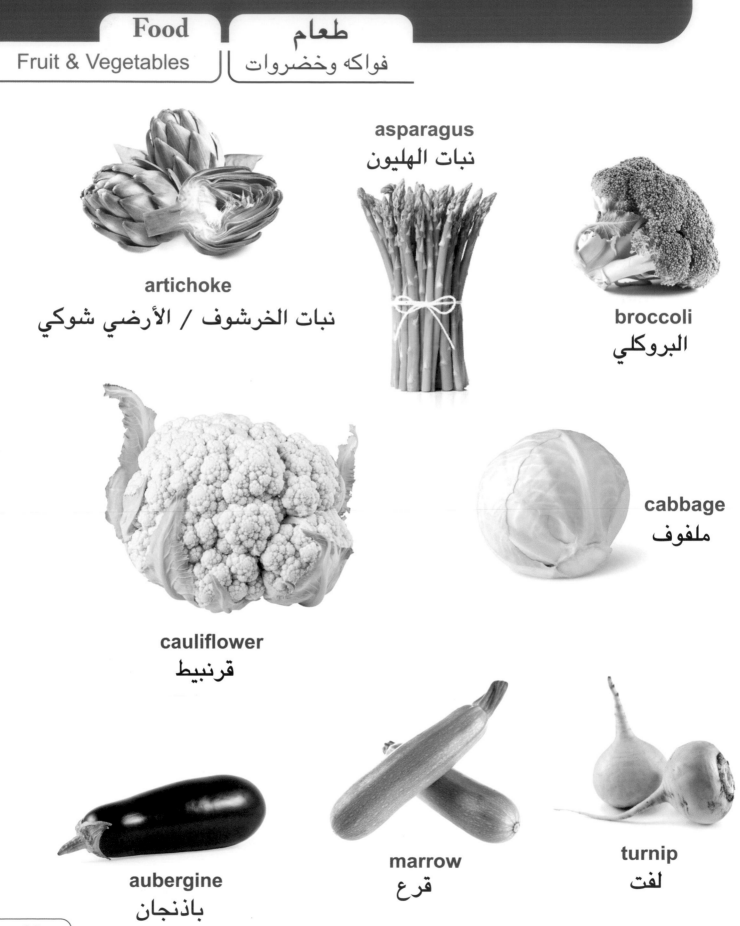

asparagus
نبات الهليون

artichoke
نبات الخرشوف / الأرضي شوكي

broccoli
البروكلي

cauliflower
قرنبيط

cabbage
ملفوف

aubergine
باذنجان

marrow
قرع

turnip
لفت

celery
كرفس

lettuce
خس

spinach
سبانخ

leek
الكرّاث

radish
فجل

spring onion
بصل أخضر

dill
الشّبت

mint
نعناع

parsley
بقدونس

61

flour

طحين

slice of bread

شريحة من الخبز

bread

خبز

crackers

بسكويت رقيق

chocolate chip cookie

كعكة مع قطع الشوكولاتة

cookie

كعكة صغيرة

toast

خبز محمص

pie
فطيرة

pizza
بيتزا

burger
برغر

sandwich
سندويتش

cake
كعكة

pancakes
فطائر

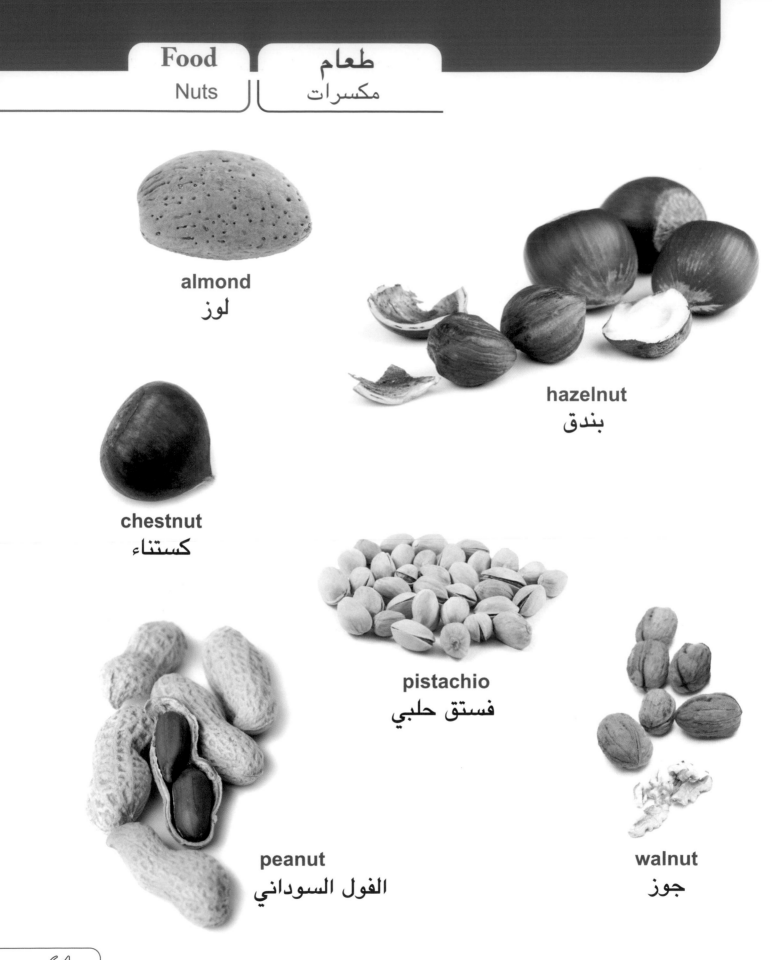

almond
لوز

hazelnut
بندق

chestnut
كستناء

pistachio
فستق حلبي

peanut
الفول السوداني

walnut
جوز

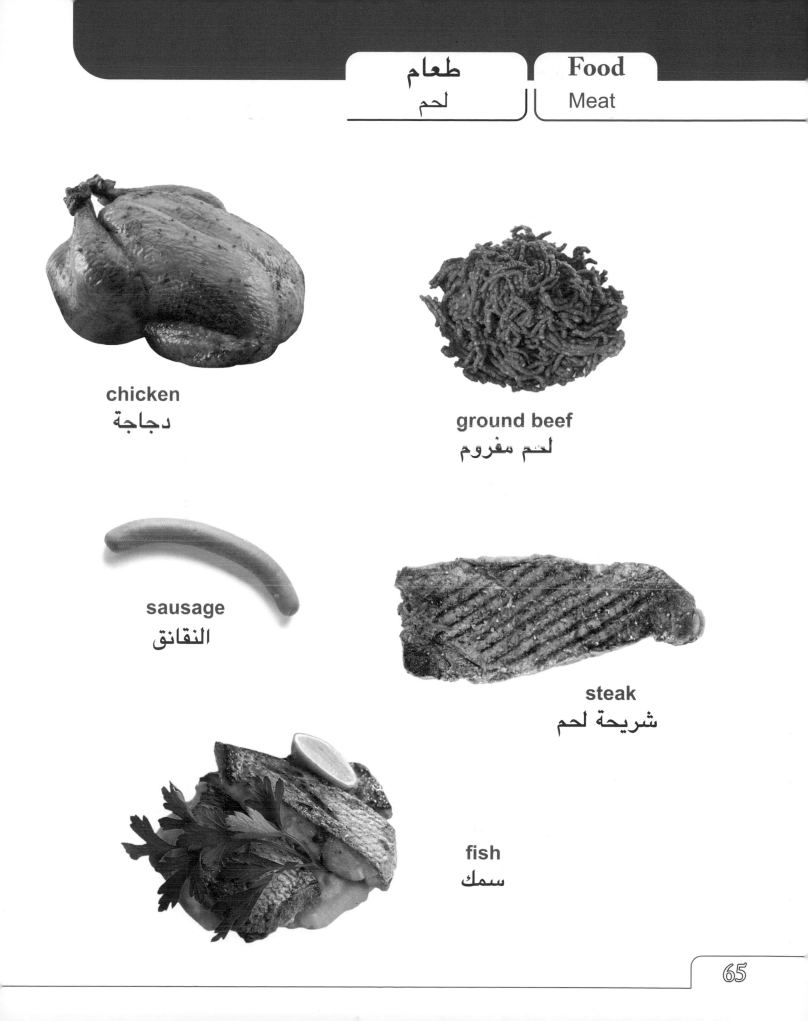

chicken
دجاجة

ground beef
لحم سفروم

sausage
النقانق

steak
شريحة لحم

fish
سمك

yolk
صفار البيض

egg
بيضة

pasta
معكرونة

rice
أرزّ

lentils
عدس

beans
فاصوليا

oil
زيت

olive oil
زيت زيتون

canned food
طعام معلّب

honey
عسل

olive
زيتون

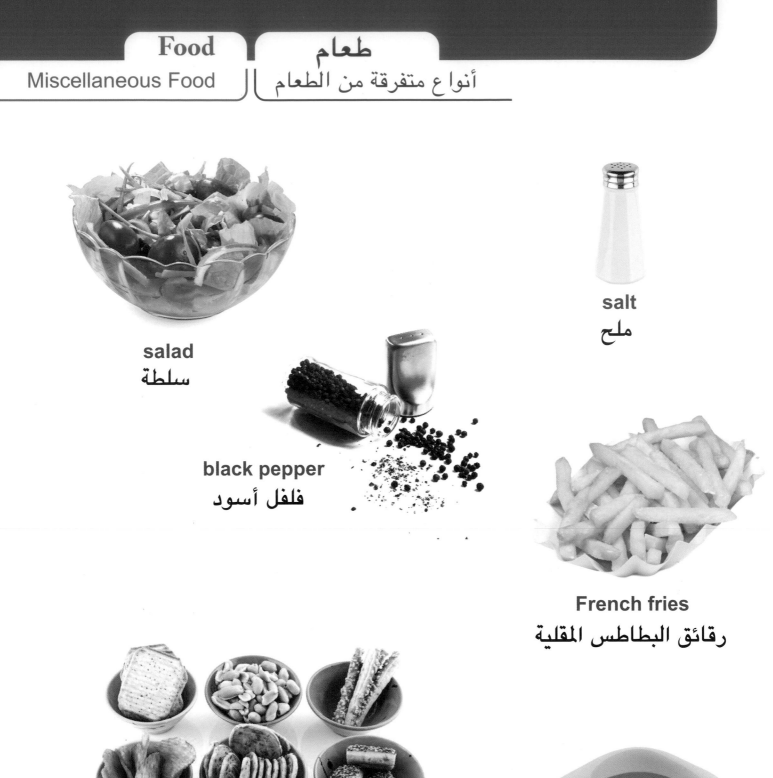

salad
سلطة

black pepper
فلفل أسود

salt
ملح

French fries
رقائق البطاطس المقلية

snacks
وجبات خفيفة

soup
حساء

candies

حلوى

breakfast

إفطار

sugar

سكر

chocolate

شوكولاتة

dessert

حلويات

ice cream

المثلّجات

popcorn

الفشار

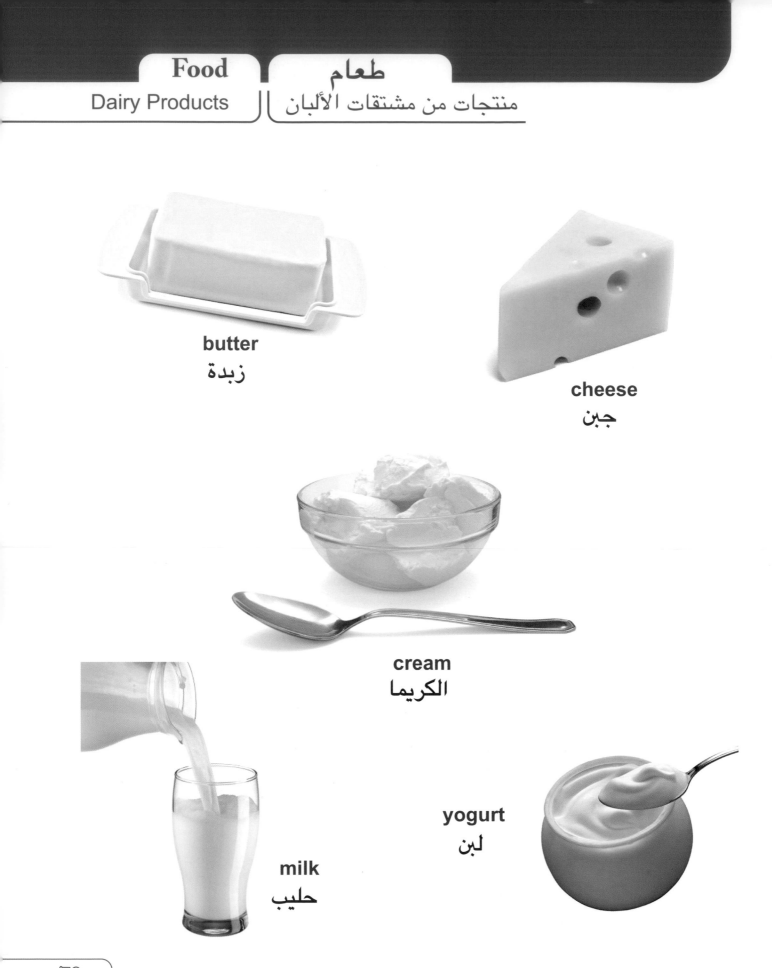

butter
زبدة

cheese
جبن

cream
الكريما

milk
حليب

yogurt
لبن

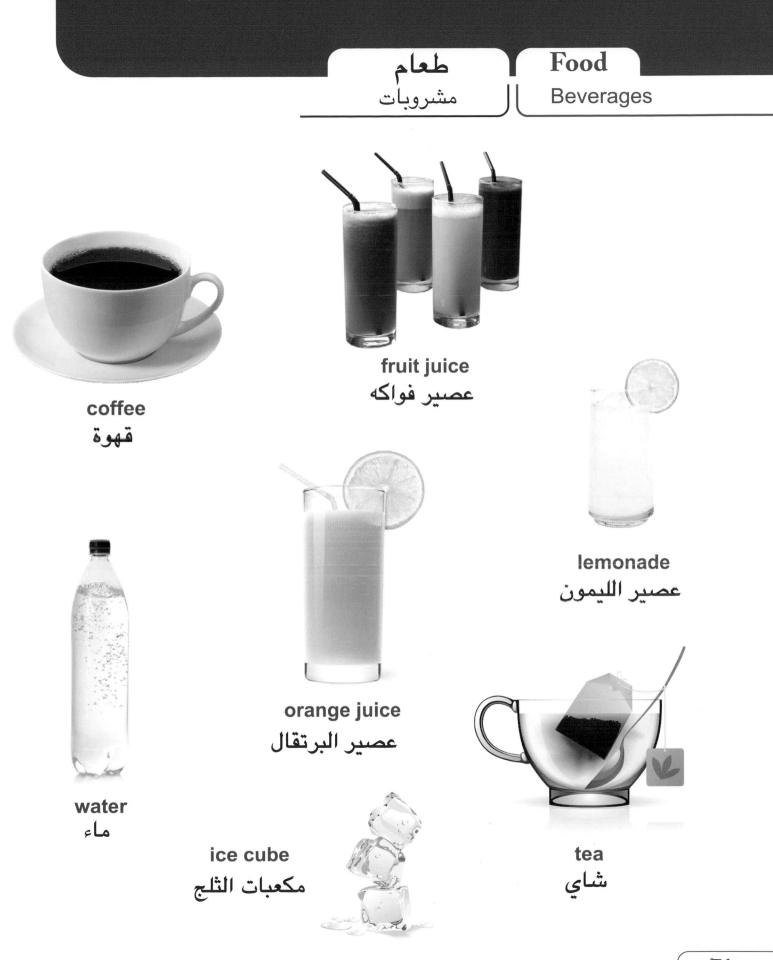

coffee
قهوة

fruit juice
عصير فواكه

lemonade
عصير الليمون

orange juice
عصير البرتقال

water
ماء

ice cube
مكعبات الثلج

tea
شاي

windscreen
الزجاج الأمامي

car
سيارة

hood
غطاء المحرك

spoke
مكبح

tire
عجلة

fender
ممتص الصدمات

headlight
مصباح السيارة الأمامي

trunk
صندوق السيارة

steering wheel
مقود

gas cap
غطاء خزان الوقود

windscreen wipers
ماسحات الزجاج

engine
محرّك

minivan

حافلة صغيرة

van

شاحنة صغيرة

camper van

عربة تخييم

pickup truck

شاحنة

dump truck

شاحنة النفايات

truck

شاحنة

transporter

شاحنة نقل

tow truck

شاحنة لسحب السيارات

bulldozer
جرافة

digger truck
شاحنة الحفر

forklift
رافعة

tractor
جرار

fire truck
سيارة إطفاء

ambulance
سيارة إسعاف

police car
سيارة شرطة

race car
سيارة سباق

bicycle
دراجة هوائية

saddle
مقعد دراجة

handlebars
مقود الدراجة

wheel
عجلة

brake
فرامل

pedal
دواسة

scooter
دراجة بخارية صغيرة

motorcycle
دراجة نارية

traffic light
إشارة مرور

stroller
عربة أطفال

rollerblade
حذاء تزلّج

sled
مزلجة

airplane
طائرة

wing
جناح الطائرة

helicopter
طائرة مروحية

flight deck
قمرة قيادة الطائرة

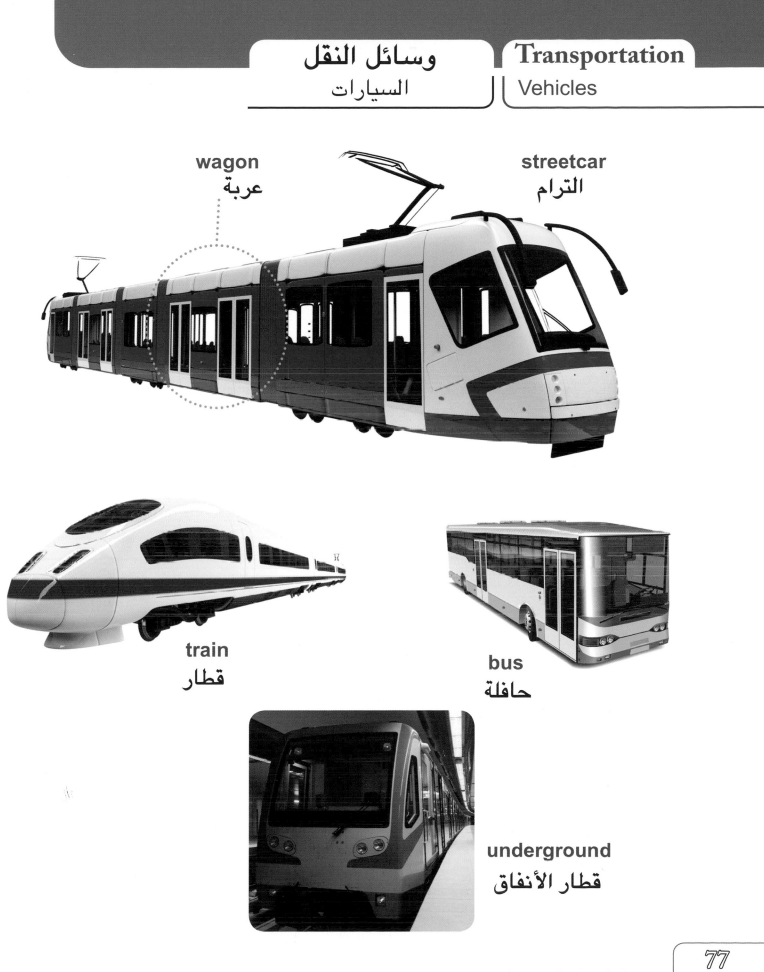

wagon
عربة

streetcar
الترام

train
قطار

bus
حافلة

underground
قطار الأنفاق

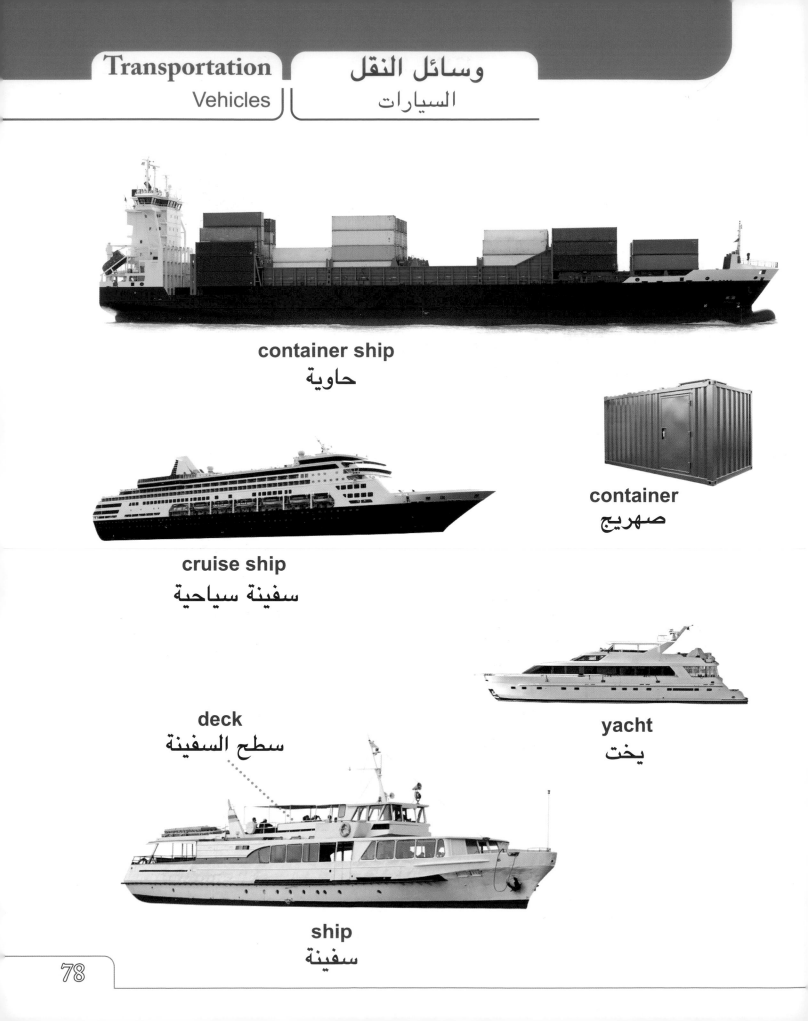

container ship
حاوية

container
صهريج

cruise ship
سفينة سياحية

yacht
يخت

deck
سطح السفينة

ship
سفينة

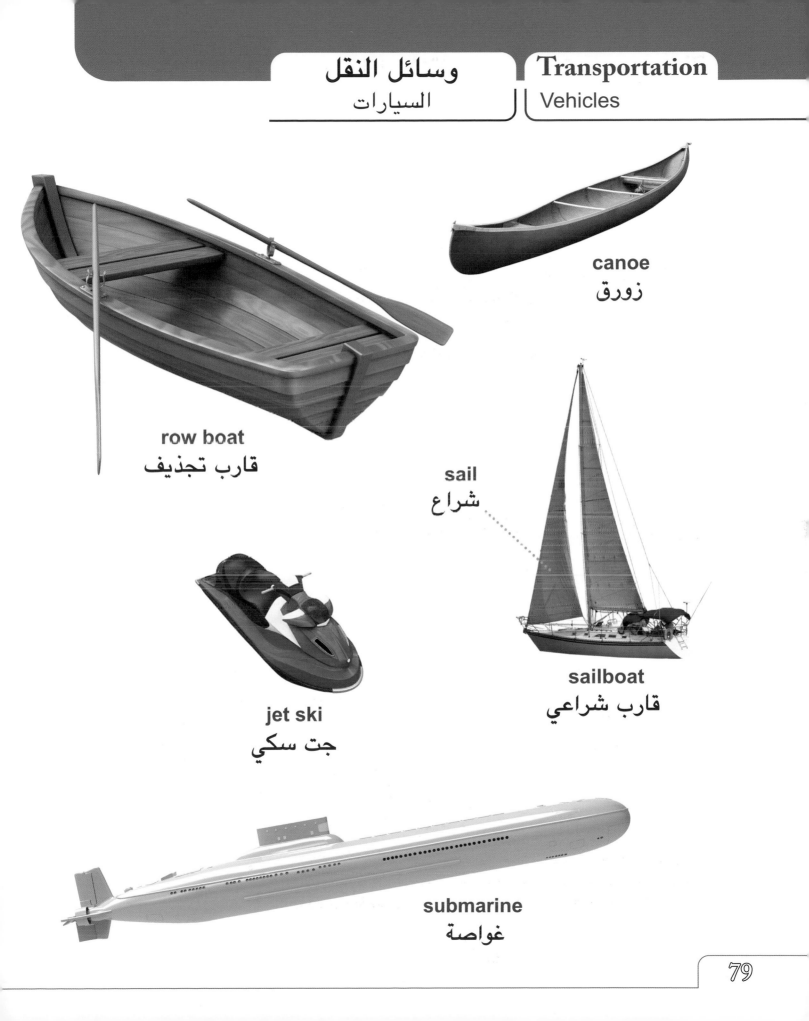

canoe

زورق

row boat

قارب تجذيف

sail

شراع

sailboat

قارب شراعي

jet ski

جت سكي

submarine

غواصة

airport

مطار

passenger terminal

قاعة الركاب

bus stop

موقف للحافلات

crosswalk

ممر مشاة

sidewalk

رصيف

street

شارع

road

طريق

highway

طريق سريع

traffic

المرور

garage

مرآب

gas station

محطة وقود

gas pump

مضخة وقود

bridge

جسر

pier

رصيف ممتد في البحر

port

ميناء

railroad station

محطة قطار

railroad track

سكة قطار

tunnel

نفق

bud

برعم

begonia

البغونية

camellia

زهرة الكاميليا

cotton

قطن

daisy

زهرة الأقحوان

carnation

زهر القرنفل

fuchsia

شجيرة الفوشية

gardenia

شجرة الغاردينيا

geranium

زهرة إبرة الراعي

iris

زهرة القزحية

hyacinth

زهرة الياقوتية

jonquil

النرجس الأسَلي

jasmine

ياسمين

lavender

الخزامى

lilac

زهر الليلك

magnolia

الماغنوليا

moss

طحالب

narcissus

زهر النرجس

nettle

نبات القُرّاص

poppy

زهرة الخشخاش

weed

عشبة ضارة

snapdragon

نبتة أنف العجل

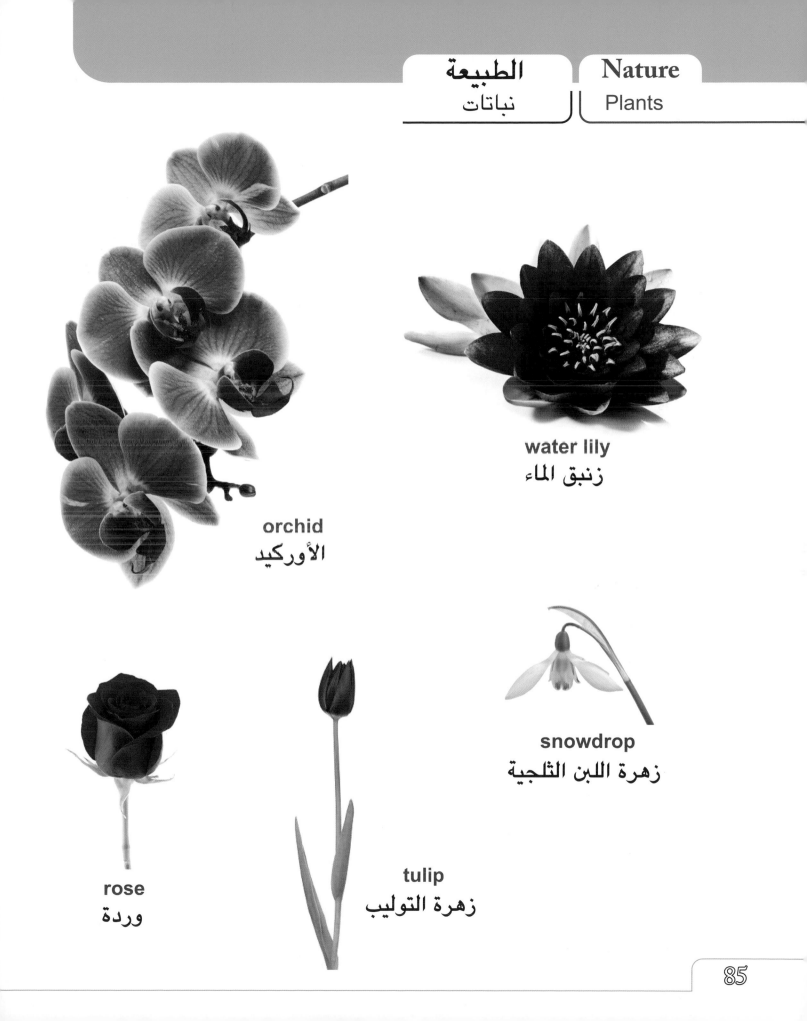

water lily
زنبق الماء

orchid
الأوركيد

snowdrop
زهرة اللبن الثلجية

rose
وردة

tulip
زهرة التوليب

sunflower
زهرة عباد الشمس

palm tree
شجرة نخيل

vineyard
كرم

rye
الجاودار

oats
الشوفان

pine cone
كوز الصنوبر

wheat
قمح

cactus
صبّار

grass
عشب

root
جذر

bush
شجيرة

stem
ساق النبات

leaf
ورقة نبات

petal
نبات البَتَلة

tree
شجرة

garden
حديقة

wood
خشب

field
حقل

log
رند الخشب

harvest
حصاد

hay
قش

beach
شاطئ

coast
ساحل

island
جزيرة

sand
رمال

ocean
محيط

marsh
مستنقع

lake
بركة

river
نهر

pebbles
حصاة

stream
جدول

waterfall
شلال

desert
صحراء

layer
طبقة

stone
حجر

clay
فخار

hill
هضبة

mountain
جبل

jungle
أدغال

forest
غابة

soil
تربة

cliff
جرف

path
ممر

valley
وادي

cave
كهف

rocky landscape
مشهد طبيعة صخرية

rock
صخرة

coal
فحم

slope
منحدر

volcano
بركان

avalanche
انهيار ثلجي

snow
ثلج

frost
جليد

icicle
كتلة ثلج مدلاة

hail
برَد

cloud
سحابة

lightning

برق

tornado

إعصار

rain

مطر

fog

ضباب

flood

طوفان

wind

رياح

Europe
أوروبا

North America
أميريكا الشمالية

South America
أميريكا الجنوبية

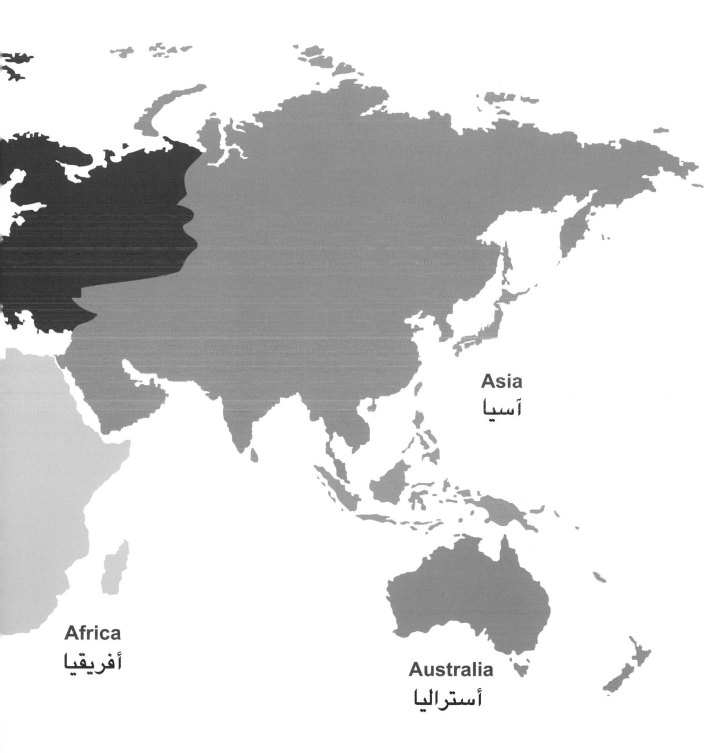

Asia
آسيا

Africa
أفريقيا

Australia
أستراليا

Earth
كوكب
الأرض

Moon
القمر

Sun
الشمس

Saturn
كوكب زحل

Venus
كوكب فينوس

Uranus
أورانوس

Jupiter
كوكب المشتري

Mars
المريخ

Mercury
كوكب عطارد

Neptune
كوكب نيبتون

galaxy
المجرة

Milky Way
درب التبانة

space
الفضاء

satellite dish
طبق الأقمار الصناعية

astronaut
رائد فضاء

space shuttle
مكوك فضائي

space station
محطة فضائية

canal
قناة مياه

dam
سد

wave
موجة

watermill
طاحونة مياه

countryside
الريف

mud
طين

puddle
بركة ماء صغيرة

disaster
كارثة

earthquake
زلزال

fire
نار

flame
لهب

ember
جمر

fossil
مستحاثة

American football
كرة القدم الأميركية

archery
الرماية

athletics
ألعاب القوى

cricket
الكريكيت

badminton
البدمنتن / تنس الريشة

cycling
ركوب الدراجات

weightlifting
رفع أثقال

basketball
كرة السلة

diving
غوص

baseball
البيسبول

hand gliding
طائرة شراعية

judo
الجودو

taekwondo
التايكوندو

wrestling
مصارعة

fencing
مبارزة بالسيف

handball
كرة اليد

high jump
الوثب العالي

golf
غولف

hurdles
سباق الحواجز

horse racing
سباق الأحصنة

horse riding
ركوب الخيل

javelin
رياضة رمي المرح

mountaineering
رياضة تسلّق الجبال

volleyball
الكرة الطائرة

rafting
رياضة التجذيف الجماعي

marathon
سباق المسافات الطويلة

rowing
تجذيف

sailing
الإبحار

water skiing
تزلج على الماء

skiing
تزلّج

snowboarding
التزلج على الجليد

ice hockey
الهوكي على الجليد

speed skating
رياضة التزلج السريع

soccer
كرة القدم

stadium
مدرج الألعاب الرياضية

table tennis
لعبة تنس الطاولة

tennis
لعبة التنس

swimming pool
حوض سباحة

swimming
السباحة

water polo
كرة الماء

compass
بوصلة

sleeping bag
كيس النوم

stopwatch
ساعة التوقيف

tent
خيمة

canvas
القنّب

palette
لوح ألوان الرسام

picture
لوحة

picture frame
إطار صورة

easel
حامل لقماشة الرسام

bust
تمثال نصفي

statue
تمثال

DONATELLO

audience

جمهور

auditorium

قاعة الاستماع

ballet

باليه

cinema

سينما

concert

حفلة موسيقية

museum

متحف

orchestra

أوركسترا

theater

مسرح

stage

خشبة المسرح

mandolin
آلة المندولين

banjo
بانجو

acoustic guitar
غيتار صوتي

electric guitar
غيتار كهربائي

balalaika
البالالايكة / آلة موسيقية
روسية تشبه الغيتار

harp
قيثارة

accordion
أكورديون

piano
بيانو

harmonica
هارمونيكا

bagpipes

مزمار القِربة

bassoon

مزمار الباسون

clarinet

كلارينيت

flute

آلة الفلوت

oboe

مزمار

saxophone

الساكسفون

trombone

المترددة، آلة موسيقية

trumpet

بوق

tuba

نوع من الأبواق

drumsticks
مضارب الطبل

cymbal
الصنج

bass drum
الطبلة العظمى

drum kit
مجموعة طبول

tambourine
دف صغير

snare drum
طبل ذو صوت حاد

timpani
دفية

cello

التشيلو / فيولونسيل

violin

كمان

double bass

الدبلبس / الكمان الكبير

music stand

حامل للنوتة الموسيقية

metronome

بندول الإيقاع

tuning fork

الشوكة الرنانة

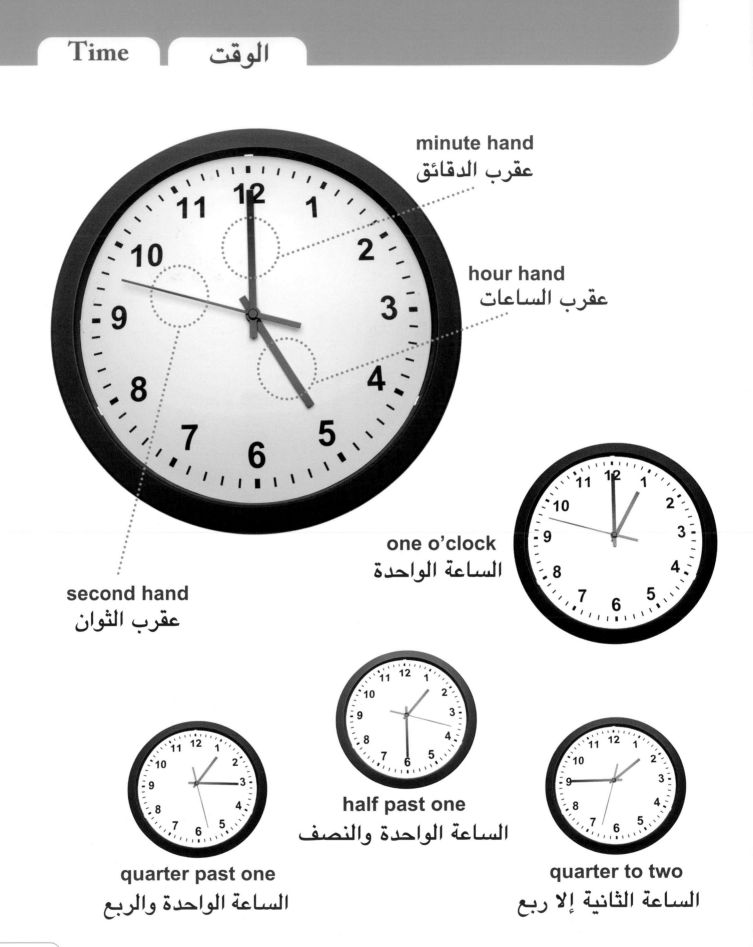

minute hand
عقرب الدقائق

hour hand
عقرب الساعات

one o'clock
الساعة الواحدة

second hand
عقرب الثوان

half past one
الساعة الواحدة والنصف

quarter past one
الساعة الواحدة والربع

quarter to two
الساعة الثانية إلا ربع

week أسبوع

2013 year سنة

January
Sun	Mon	Tue	Wed	Thu	Fri	Sat
30	31	1	2	3	4	5
6	7	8	9	10	11	12
13	14	15	16	17	18	19
20	21	22	23	24	25	26
27	28	29	30	31	1	2
3	4	5	6	7	8	9

February
Sun	Mon	Tue	Wed	Thu	Fri	Sat
27	28	29	30	31	1	2
3	4	5	6	7	8	9
10	11	12	13	14	15	16
17	18	19	20	21	22	23
24	25	26	27	28	1	2
3	4	5	6	7	8	9

March
Sun	Mon	Tue	Wed	Thu	Fri	Sat
24	25	26	27	28	1	2
3	4	5	6	7	8	9
10	11	12	13	14	15	16
17	18	19	20	21	22	23
24	25	26	27	28	29	30
31	1	2	3	4	5	6

April
Sun	Mon	Tue	Wed	Thu	Fri	Sat
31	1	2	3	4	5	6
7	8	9	10	11	12	13
14	15	16	17	18	19	20
21	22	23	24	25	26	27
28	29	30	1	2	3	4
5	6	7	8	9	10	11

May
Sun	Mon	Tue	Wed	Thu	Fri	Sat
28	29	30	1	2	3	4
5	6	7	8	9	10	11
12	13	14	15	16	17	18
19	20	21	22	23	24	25
26	27	28	29	30	31	1
2	3	4	5	6	7	8

June
Sun	Mon	Tue	Wed	Thu	Fri	Sat
26	27	28	29	30	31	1
2	3	4	5	6	7	8
9	10	11	12	13	14	15
16	17	18	19	20	21	22
23	24	25	26	27	28	29
30	1	2	3	4	5	6

month شهر

fortnight أسبوعين

July
Sun	Mon	Tue	Wed	Thu	Fri	Sat
30	1	2	3	4	5	6
7	8	9	10	11	12	13
14	15	16	17	18	19	20
21	22	23	24	25	26	27
28	29	30	31	1	2	3
4	5	6	7	8	9	10

August
Sun	Mon	Tue	Wed	Thu	Fri	Sat
28	29	30	31	1	2	3
4	5	6	7	8	9	10
11	12	13	14	15	16	17
18	19	20	21	22	23	24
25	26	27	28	29	30	31
1	2	3	4	5	6	7

September
Sun	Mon	Tue	Wed	Thu	Fri	Sat
1	2	3	4	5	6	7
8	9	10	11	12	13	14
15	16	17	18	19	20	21
22	23	24	25	26	27	28
29	30	1	2	3	4	5
6	7	8	9	10	11	12

October
Sun	Mon	Tue	Wed	Thu	Fri	Sat
29	30	1	2	3	4	5
6	7	8	9	10	11	12
13	14	15	16	17	18	19
20	21	22	23	24	25	26
27	28	29	30	31	1	2
3	4	5	6	7	8	9

November
Sun	Mon	Tue	Wed	Thu	Fri	Sat
27	28	29	30	31	1	2
3	4	5	6	7	8	9
10	11	12	13	14	15	16
17	18	19	20	21	22	23
24	25	26	27	28	29	30
1	2	3	4	5	6	7

December
Sun	Mon	Tue	Wed	Thu	Fri	Sat
1	2	3	4	5	6	7
8	9	10	11	12	13	14
15	16	17	18	19	20	21
22	23	24	25	26	27	28
29	30	31	1	2	3	4
5	6	7	8	9	10	11

10 YEARS ANNIVERSARY
decade عقد

100 YEARS
century قرن

1000 YEARS
millennium ألفية

spring
فصل الربيع

summer
فصل الصيف

fall
فصل الخريف

winter
فصل الشتاء

sunrise
الشروق

dawn
فجر

dusk
غسق

evening
مساء

night
ليل

midnight
منتصف الليل

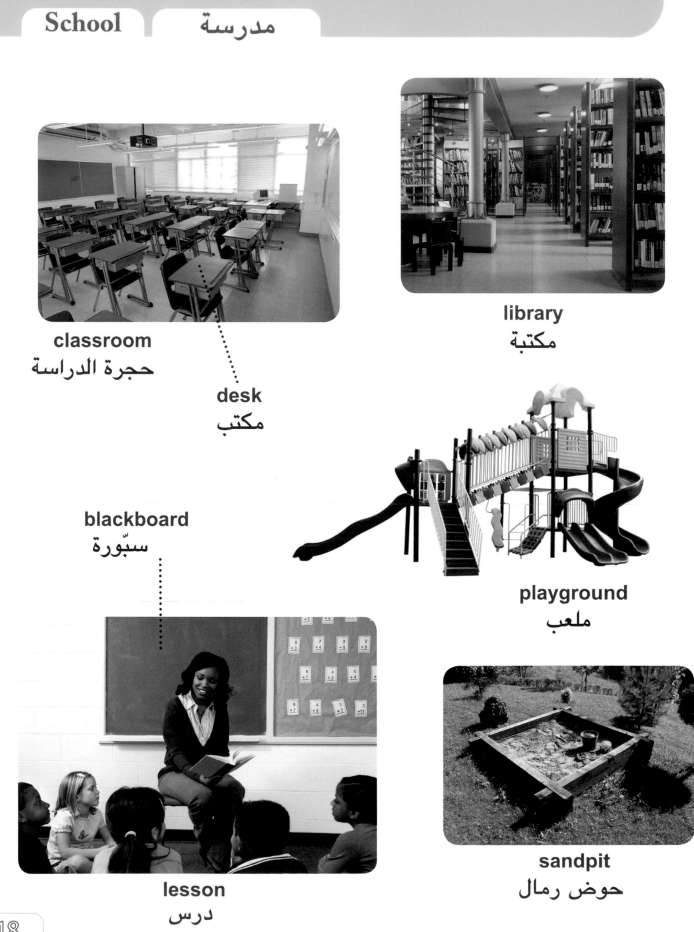

classroom
حجرة الدراسة

desk
مكتب

library
مكتبة

blackboard
سبّورة

playground
ملعب

lesson
درس

sandpit
حوض رمال

page
صفحة

pen
قلم حبر

abacus
معداد

notebook
مفكرة

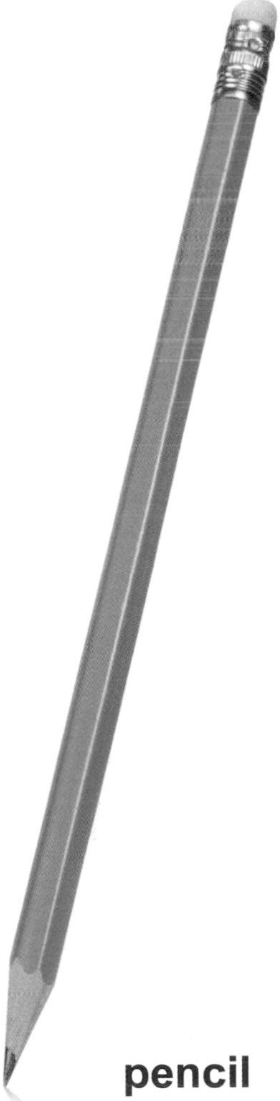

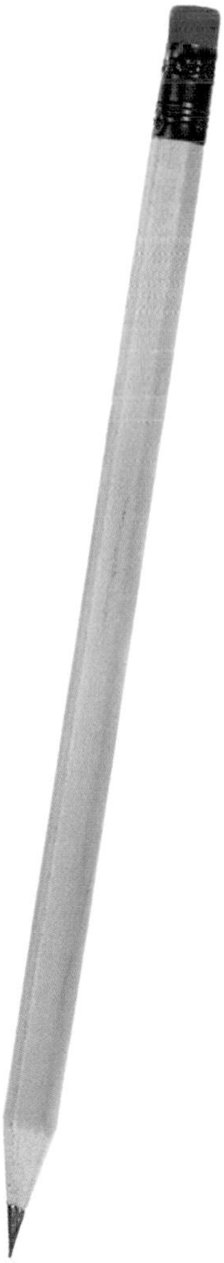

ballpoint pen
قلم حبر جاف

pencil sharpener
المبراة

pencil
قلم رصاص

eraser
ممحاة

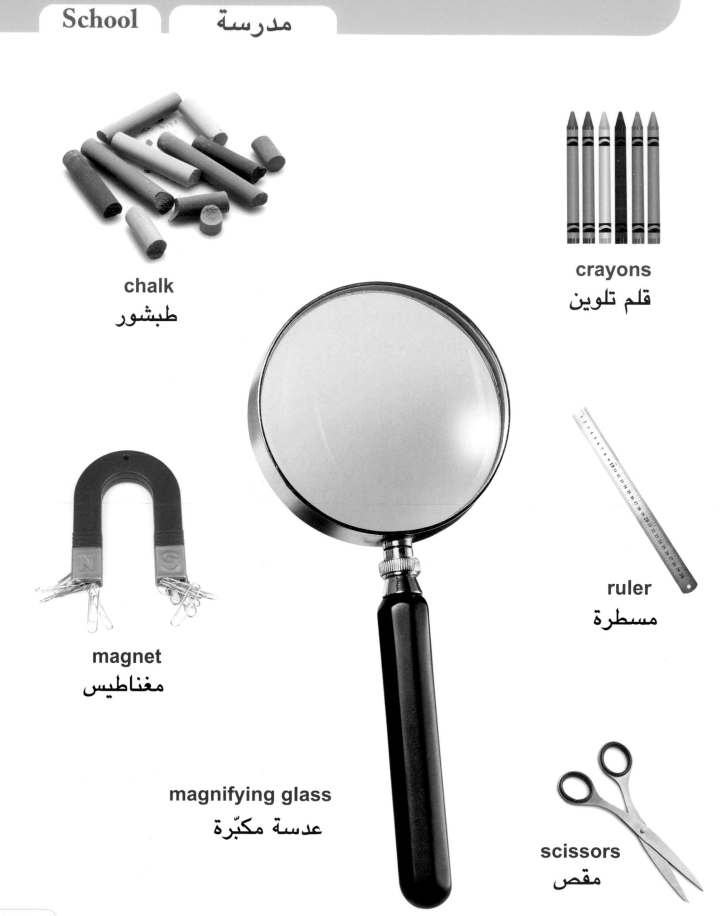

chalk
طبشور

crayons
قلم تلوين

ruler
مسطرة

magnet
مغناطيس

magnifying glass
عدسة مكبّرة

scissors
مقص

pushpin
دبوس تثبيت

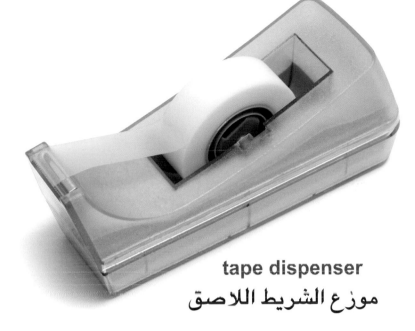

tape dispenser
موزع الشريط اللاصق

paper-clip
مشبك أوراق

globe
الكرة الأرضية

telescope
منظار

microscope
مجهر

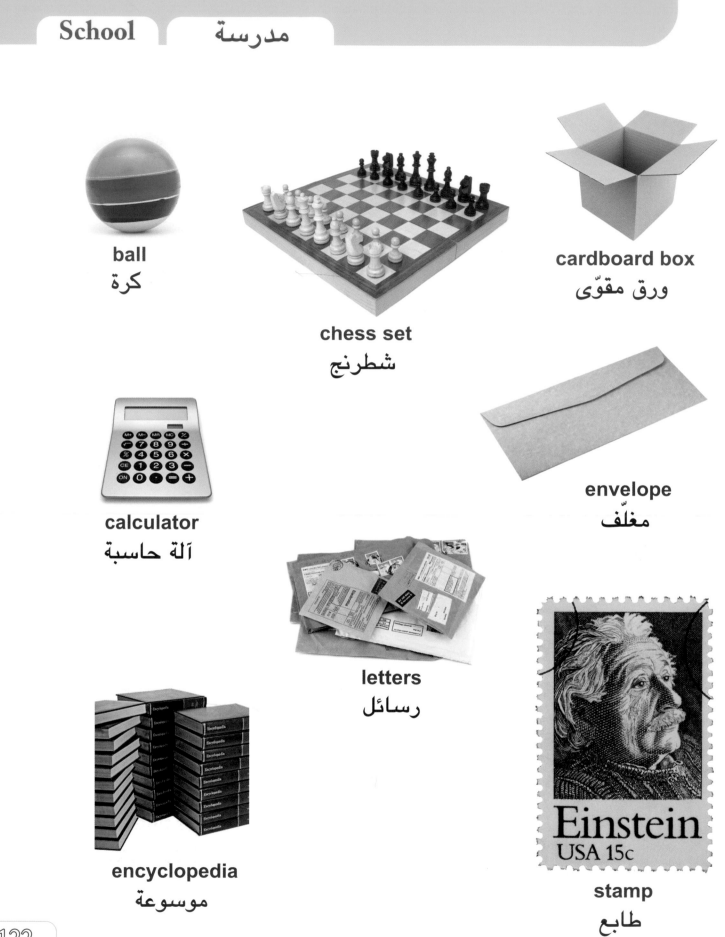

ball
كرة

chess set
شطرنج

cardboard box
ورق مقوّى

calculator
آلة حاسبة

envelope
مغلَّف

letters
رسائل

encyclopedia
موسوعة

stamp
طابع

ink
حبر

hole puncher
مكبس ثقب الورق

rubber stamp
ختم

staple remover
مزيل مشبك الورق

stapler
كباس الورق

staples
مشبك ورق سلكي

waste basket
سلة مهملات

whistle
صافرة

writing pad
مسند للكتابة

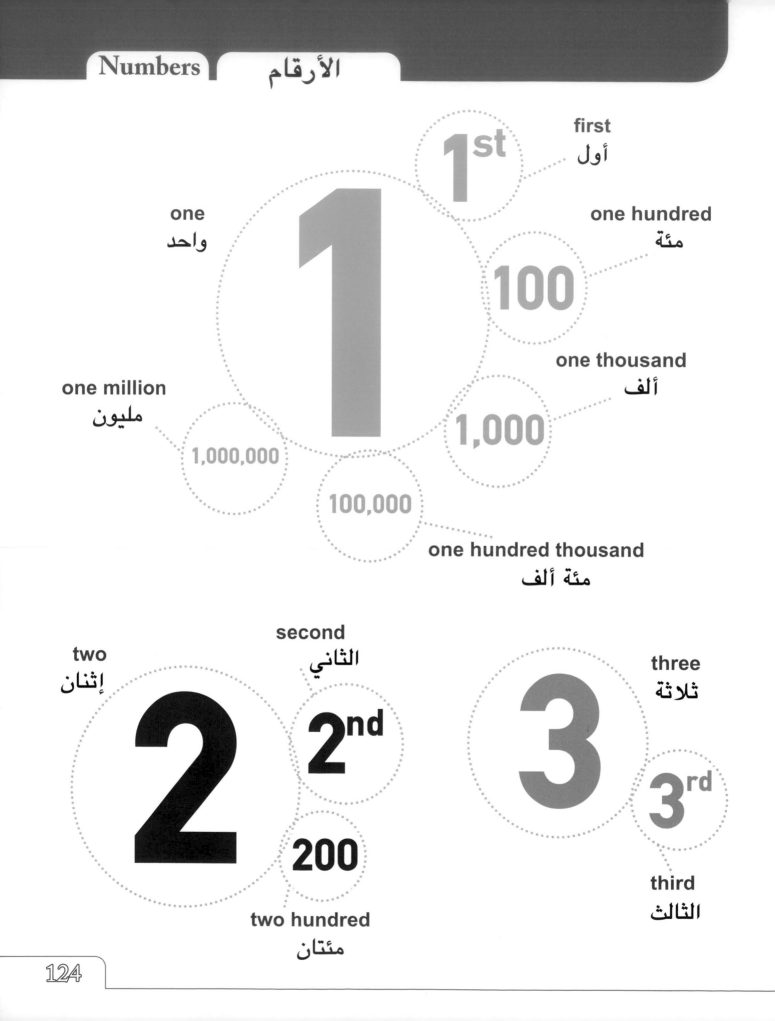

first
أول
1st

one
واحد
1

one hundred
مئة
100

one thousand
ألف
1,000

one million
مليون
1,000,000

one hundred thousand
مئة ألف
100,000

two
إثنان

second
الثاني
2nd

200
two hundred
مئتان

three
ثلاثة
3

3rd
third
الثالث

four
أربعة

fourth
الرابع

4th

5

5th

five
خمسة

fifth
الخامس

six
ستة

6

sixth
السادس

6th

7

eight
ثمانية

eighth
الثامن

8th

8

7th

seven
سبعة

seventh
السابع

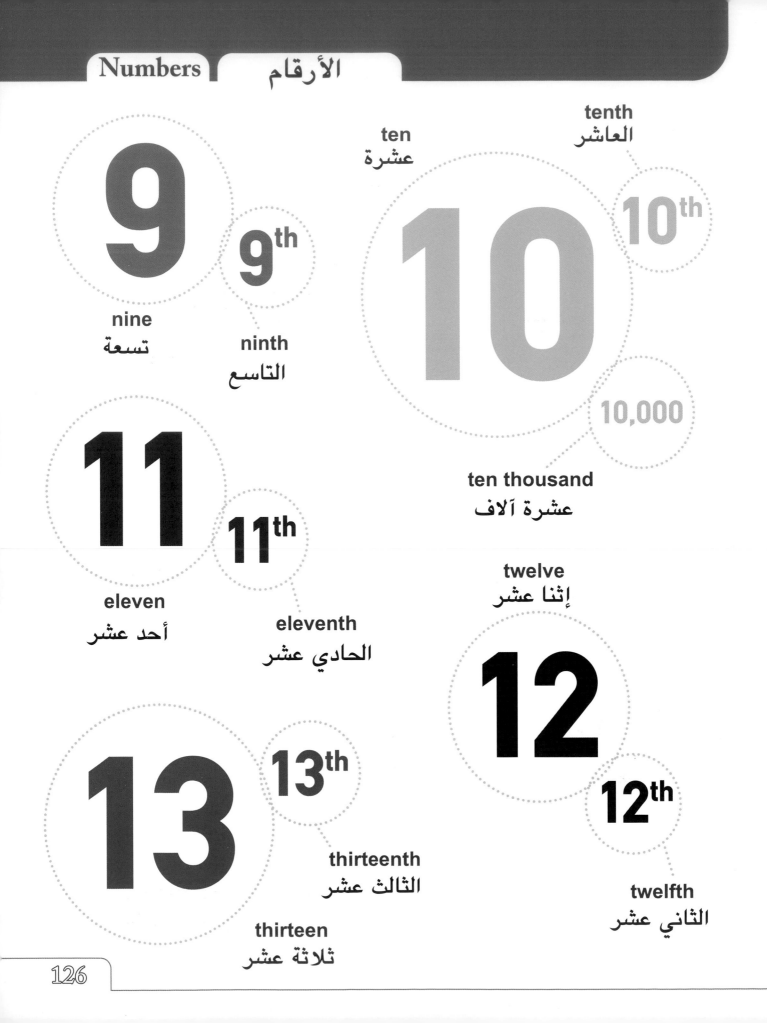

9

9th

nine
تسعة

ninth
التاسع

10

tenth
العاشر

ten
عشرة

10th

10,000

ten thousand
عشرة آلاف

11

11th

eleven
أحد عشر

eleventh
الحادي عشر

twelve
إثنا عشر

12

12th

twelfth
الثاني عشر

13

13th

thirteenth
الثالث عشر

thirteen
ثلاثة عشر

126

fourteen
أربعة عشر

14

14th

fourteenth
الرابع عشر

fifteen
خمسة عشر

15

15th

fifteenth
الخامس عشر

sixteen
ستة عشر

16

16th

sixteenth
السادس عشر

17

17th

seventeen
سبعة عشر

seventeenth
السابع عشر

eighteen
ثمانية عشر

18

18th

eighteenth
الثامن عشر

nineteen
تسعة عشر

19

19th

nineteen
التاسع عشر

20

20th twentieth العشرون

twenty عشرون

21 twenty-one واحد وعشرون

21st twenty-first الواحد والعشرون

30 thirty ثلاثون

31 thirty-one واحد وثلاثون

40 forty أربعون

41 forty-one واحد وأربعون

50 fifty خمسون

51 fifty-one واحد وخمسون

60
sixty
ستون

61
sixty-one
واحد وستون

70
seventy
سبعون

71
seventy-one
واحد وسبعون

80
eighty
ثمانون

81
eighty-one
واحد وثمانون

0
zero
صفر

90
ninety
تسعون

91
ninety-one
واحد وتسعون

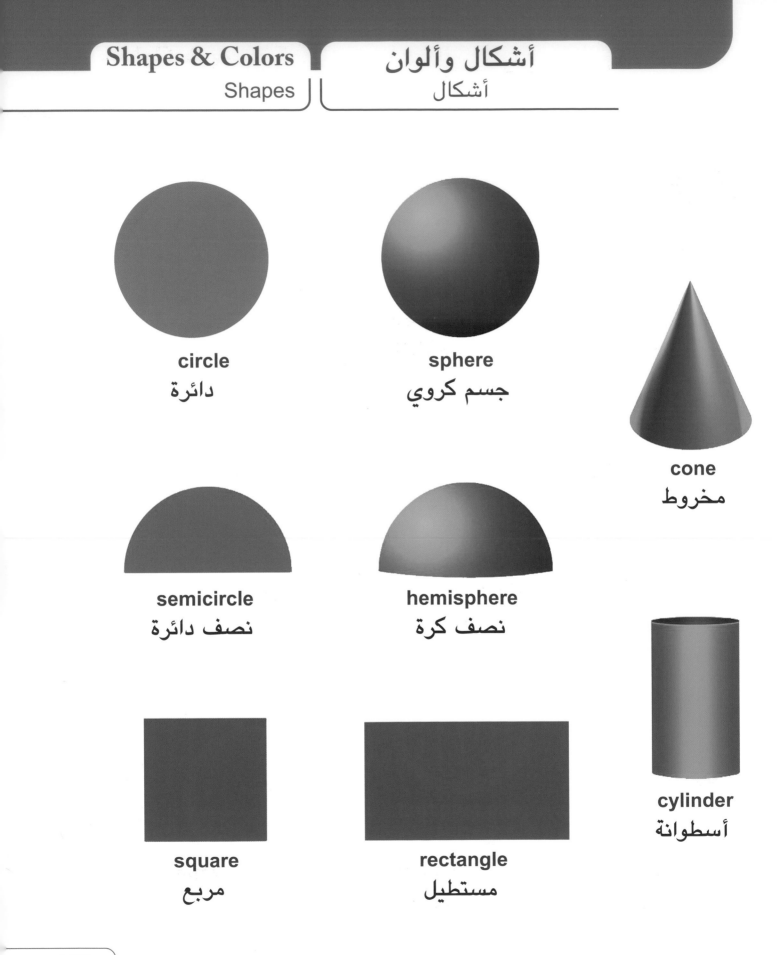

circle

دائرة

sphere

جسم كروي

cone

مخروط

semicircle

نصف دائرة

hemisphere

نصف كرة

cylinder

أسطوانة

square

مربع

rectangle

مستطيل

أشكال

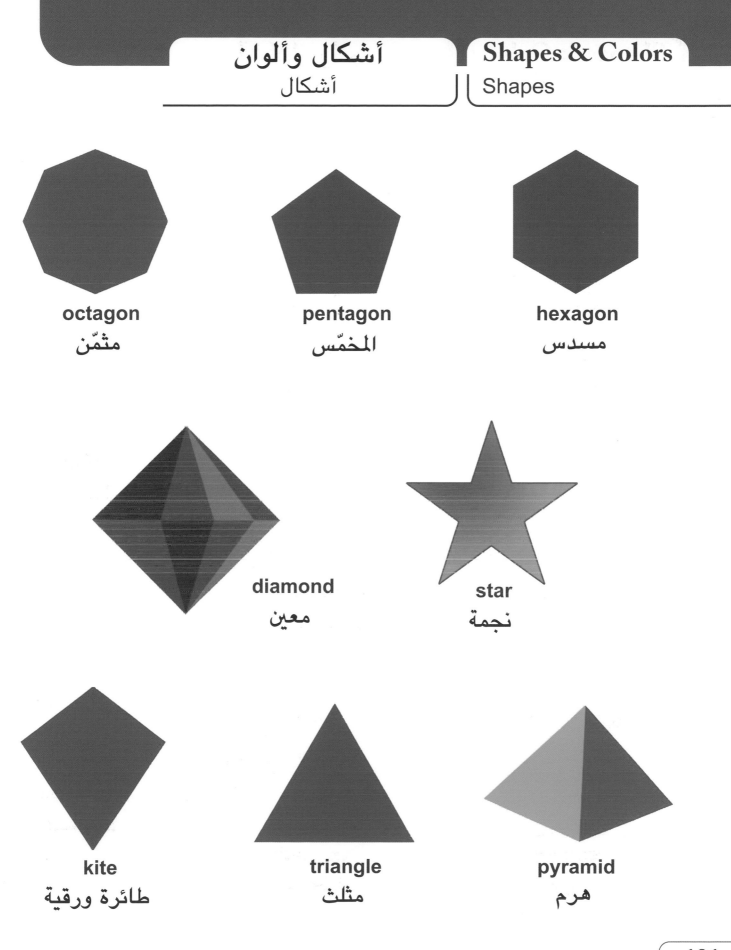

octagon
مثمّن

pentagon
المخمّس

hexagon
مسدس

diamond
معين

star
نجمة

kite
طائرة ورقية

triangle
مثلث

pyramid
هرم

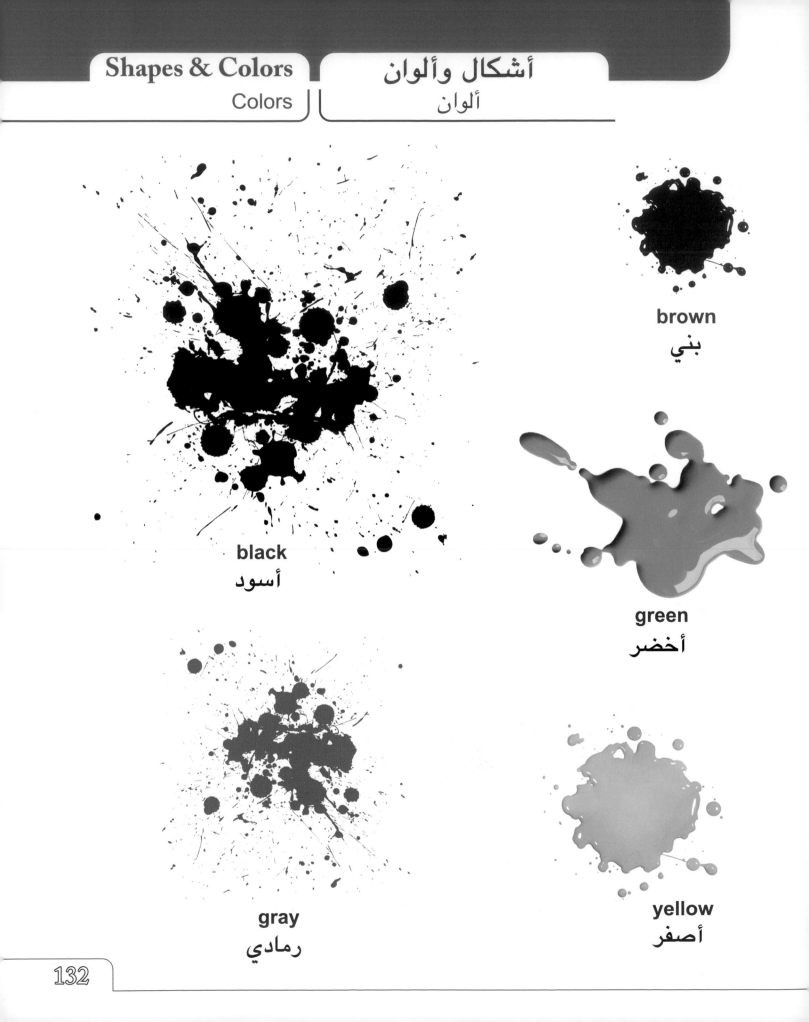

brown
بني

black
أسود

green
أخضر

gray
رمادي

yellow
أصفر

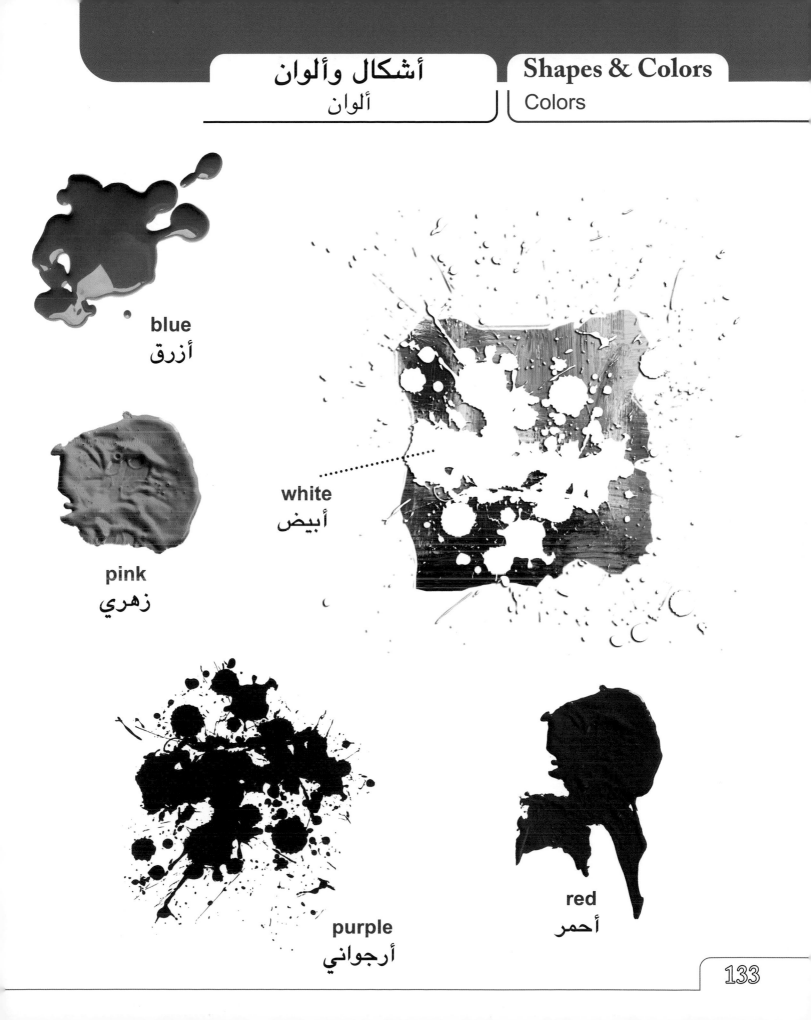

blue
أزرق

pink
زهري

white
أبيض

purple
أرجواني

red
أحمر

It's
apostrophe
الفاصلة العليا

near,
comma
فاصلة

look:
colon
نقطتان

-around-
dash
قاطعة

the...
ellipsis
علامة الحذف في الكتابة

clock!
exclamation mark
إشارة تعجب

really?
question mark
إشارة استفهام

"he said"
quotation marks
علامات الاقتباس

Yes.
period
نقطة

(almost)
parentheses
قوسان بين الكلام

done;
semicolon
فارزة منقوطة

'sir'
single quotation marks
علامات اقتباس مفردة

3+1
plus sign
إشارة الجمع

√16
square root of
الجذر التربيعي

7-3
minus sign
إشارة الطرح

25%
percent
في المئة

2×2
multiplication sign
إشارة الضرب

=4
equal sign
علامة المساواة

8÷2
division sign
علامة التقسيم

ampersand
حرف عطف

He/She
forward slash
مائل

html\n
backslash
مائل

info@milet.com
at sign
علامة @

A__abacus	119	معداد
accordion	110	أكورديون
acoustic guitar	110	غيتار صوتي
adjustable wrench	48	مفتاح ربط قابل للتعديل
Africa	97	أفريقيا
air conditioner	24	مكيف هواء
airplane	76	طائرة
airport	80	مطار
almond	64	لوز
ambulance	74	سيارة إسعاف
American football	102	كرة القدم الأميركية
ampersand	134	حرف عطف
ankle	23	كاحل
answering machine	52	جهاز استقبال المكالمات الهاتفية
ant	10	نملة
apostrophe	134	الفاصلة العليا
apple	55	تفاح
apricot	55	مشمش
archery	102	الرماية
arm	21	ذراع
armchair	25	كرسي ذو ذراعين
armpit	21	إبط
artichoke	60	نبات الخرشوف / الأرضي شوكي
Asia	97	آسيا
asparagus	60	نبات الهليون
astronaut	99	رائد فضاء
at sign	135	علامة @
athletics	102	ألعاب القوى
attic	24	عليّة
aubergine	60	باذنجان
audience	109	جمهور
auditorium	109	قاعة الاستماع
Australia	97	أستراليا
avalanche	94	انهيار ثلجي
avocado	55	أفوكادو
axe	51	فأس
B__backpack	43	حقيبة ظهر
backslash	135	مائل
badge	43	شارة انتساب
badminton	102	البدمنتن / تنس الريشة
bagpipes	111	مزمار القربة
balalaika	110	البالالايكة / آلة موسيقية روسية تشبه الغيتار
ball	122	كرة
ballet	109	باليه
ballpoint pen	119	قلم حبر جاف
banana	55	موز
banjo	110	بانجو
barn	7	إسطبل
baseball	103	البيسبول
basket	32	سلة
basketball	103	كرة السلة
bass drum	112	الطبلة العظمى
bassoon	111	مزمار الباسون
bat	16	خفاش
bathrobe	38	برنس حمام
bathroom	27	حمام
bathtub	27	حوض استحمام
battery	49	بطارية
beach	89	شاطئ
beak	4	منقار

beans	66	فاصوليا
bear	16	دب
bed	26	سرير
bedroom	26	غرفة نوم
bedside lamp	34	مصباح جانب السرير
bee	11	نحلة
beehive	11	قفير
beetle	10	خنفساء
begonia	82	البغونية
belt	40	حزام
beret	40	البيريه / قبعة مستديرة
bicycle	75	دراجة هوائية
black	132	أسود
black pepper	68	فلفل أسود
blackberry	55	ثمر العلّيق
blackboard	118	سبّورة
blanket	26	بطانية
blender	36	خلاط
blouse	39	بُلوزة
blue	133	أزرق
blueberry	55	ثمر العنبيّة
boots	41	حذاء طويل الرقبة / جزمة
bottle	30	زجاجة
bow tie	40	عقدة عنق أنشوطية
bowl	29	زبدية
box	32	صندوق
bracelet	42	سوار
brake	75	فرامل
bread	52	خبز
breakfast	69	إفطار
bridge	81	جسر
briefcase	43	حقيبة جلدية
broccoli	60	البروكلي
broom	32	مكنسة
brown	132	بني
bucket	32	دلو
bud	82	برعم
bull	7	ثور
bulldozer	74	جرافة
burger	63	برغر
burner	31	موقد
bus	77	حافلة
bus stop	80	موقف للحافلات
bush	87	شجيرة
bust	108	تمثال نصفي
butter	70	زبدة
butterfly	10	فراشة
button	44	زر
C__cabbage	60	ملفوف
cabinet	28	خزانة
cable	53	سلك
cactus	87	صبّار
cage	4	قفص
cake	63	كعكة
calculator	122	آلة حاسبة
calf	7	عجل
calf	23	بطة الساق / ربلة الساق
camel	9	جمل
camellia	82	زهرة الكاميليا
camper van	73	عربة تخييم

English	Page	Arabic
canal	100	قناة مياه
candies	69	حلوى
candle	32	شمعة
canned food	67	طعام معلّب
canoe	79	زورق
canvas	108	قماش القنّب
cap	40	قبعة
car	72	سيارة
car battery	49	بطارية السيارة
cardboard box	122	ورق مقوّى
cardigan	39	سترة من الصوف المحبوك
carnation	82	زهر القرنفل
carpet	25	سجادة
carrot	58	جزر
cat	7	قطة
caterpillar	10	يرقانة الفراشة
cauliflower	60	قرنبيط
cave	93	كهف
ceiling	25	سقف
ceiling fan	34	مروحة سقف
celery	61	كرفس
cello	113	التشيلو / فيولونسيل
century	115	قرن
chain	50	سلسلة
chair	28	كرسي
chalk	120	طبشور
chameleon	12	حرباء
chandelier	34	ثريّا
checkout	54	دفع الحساب والمغادرة
cheek	22	خد / وجنة
cheese	70	جين
cherry	55	كرز
chess set	122	شطرنج
chest	21	صدر
chestnut	64	كستناء
chick	8	صوص
chicken	65	دجاجة
chili pepper	58	فلفل حار
chimney	24	مدخنة
chimpanzee	17	الشمبانزي
chin	22	ذقن
chip	52	رقاقة إلكترونية
chisel	51	إزميل
chocolate	69	شوكولاتة
chocolate chip cookie	62	كعكة مع قطع الشوكولاتة
cinema	109	سينما
circle	130	دائرة
clarinet	111	كلارينيت
classroom	118	حجرة الدراسة
claw	4	مخلب
clay	91	فخار
cliff	92	جرف
clock	32	ساعة حائط
cloth	44	قطعة قماش / خرقة
clothes brush	44	فرشاة الملابس
clothes hanger	44	شماعة ملابس
clothes peg	32	ملقط غسيل
cloud	94	سحابة
coal	93	فحم
coast	89	ساحل
cobweb	11	شبكة العنكبوت
coconut	57	جوز الهند
cocoon	10	شرنقة
coffee	71	قهوة
collar	8	طوق
colon	134	نقطتان
comb	45	مشط
combination wrenches	48	مفتاح براغي
comforter	26	لحاف
comma	134	فاصلة
compass	107	بوصلة
computer	52	كومبيوتر
concert	109	حفلة موسيقية
cone	130	مخروط
container	78	صهريج
container ship	78	حاوية
cookie	62	كعكة صغيرة
coral	15	مرجان
corn	58	ذرة
corncob	58	كوز الذرة
cotton	82	قطن
countryside	100	الريف
cow	7	بقرة
crab	14	سرطان
crackers	62	بسكويت رقيق
crayfish	14	جراد البحر
crayons	120	قلم تلوين
cream	70	الكريما
crest	8	عرف الديك
cricket	10	الجدجد
cricket	102	الكريكيت
crocodile	12	تمساح
crosswalk	80	ممر مشاة
crow	4	غراب
cruise ship	78	سفينة سياحية
cub	18	جرو الثعلب
cucumber	59	خيار
curtain	25	ستارة
cushion	25	وسادة
cutting board	31	لوح لتقطيع الطعام
cycling	102	ركوب الدراجات
cylinder	130	أسطوانة
cymbal	112	الصنج
D daisy	82	زهرة الأقحوان
dam	100	سد
dash	134	قاطعة
dawn	117	فجر
decade	115	عقد
deck	78	سطح السفينة
deep fryer	35	مقلاة عميقة
deer	19	الأيل
desert	91	صحراء
desk	118	مكتب
desk lamp	34	مصباح المكتب
dessert	69	حلويات
diamond	42	الماس
diamond	131	معين
digger truck	74	شاحنة الحفر
dill	61	الشبّت
dining table	28	مائدة طعام

disaster	101	كارثة	eyelashes	22	رموش
dishwasher	37	غسالة صحون	eyelid	22	جفن
diving	103	غوص	**F** _ face	22	وجه
division sign	135	علامة التقسيم	falcon	4	صقر
dog	7	كلب	fall	116	فصل الخريف
doghouse	7	بيت الكلب	faucet	31	صنبور
dolphin	14	دلفين	fawn	19	الخشف ولد الظبي
donkey	9	حمار	feather	4	ريشة
door	24	باب	fencing	104	مبارزة بالسيف
door handle	36	مقبض الباب	fender	72	ممتص الصدمات
doorbell	36	جرس الباب	field	88	حقل
doormat	33	ممسحة الأرجل	fifteen	127	خمسة عشر
double bass	113	الدبلس / الكمان الكبير	fifteenth	127	الخامس عشر
dragonfly	10	يَعسوب	fifth	125	الخامس
dress	38	فستان	fifty	128	خمسون
drill bit	49	جزء المثقب اللولبي	fifty-one	128	واحد وخمسون
drum kit	112	مجموعة طبول	fingerprint	23	بصمة
drumsticks	112	مضارب الطبل	fire	101	نار
duck	8	بطة	fire extinguisher	50	مطفئة حريق
dump truck	73	شاحنة النفايات	fire truck	74	سيارة إطفاء
dusk	117	غسق	fireplace	25	مدفأة
E _ eagle	4	نسر	first	124	أول
ear	22	أذن	fish	14	سمكة
earphones	53	سماعات الأذن	fish	65	سمك
earrings	42	قرط	five	125	خمسة
Earth	98	كوكب الأرض	flame	101	لهب
earthquake	101	زلزال	flamingo	4	طائر البشروس
earthworm	13	دودة الأرض	flight deck	76	قمرة قيادة الطائرة
easel	108	حامل لقماشة الرسام	flip-flops	41	شبشب
egg	4	بيضة	flood	95	طوفان
egg	66	بيضة	floor	25	أرضية
eight	125	ثمانية	floor lamp	34	مصباح الأرضية
eighteen	127	ثمانية عشر	flour	62	طحين
eighteenth	127	الثامن عشر	flowerpot	33	إناء زهور
eighth	125	الثامن	flute	111	آلة الفلوت
eighty	129	ثمانون	fly	11	ذبابة
eighty-one	129	واحد وثمانون	fog	95	ضباب
elbow	23	مرفق	folding chair	25	كرسي قابل للطي
electric cooker	35	موقد كهربائي	food processor	36	آلة لإعداد الطعام
electric drill	49	مثقب كهربائي	foot	21	قدم
electric guitar	110	غيتار كهربائي	footprint	21	أثر القدم
electric razor	46	ماكينة حلاقة كهربائية	forehead	21	جبين
electrical outlet	36	مأخذ التيار الكهربائي	forest	92	غابة
elephant	16	فيل	fork	30	شوكة
eleven	126	أحد عشر	forklift	74	رافعة
eleventh	126	الحادي عشر	fortnight	115	أسبوعين
ellipsis	134	علامة الحذف في الكتابة	forty	128	أربعون
ember	101	جمر	forty-one	128	واحد وأربعون
emerald	42	زمرد	forward slash	135	مائل
encyclopedia	122	موسوعة	fossil	101	مستحاثة
engine	72	محرّك	foulard	40	وشاح حريري
envelope	122	مغلف	four	125	أربعة
equal sign	135	علامة المساواة	fourteen	127	أربعة عشر
eraser	119	ممحاة	fourteenth	127	الرابع عشر
Europe	96	أوروبا	fourth	125	الرابع
evening	117	مساء	fox	17	ثعلب
exclamation mark	134	إشارة تعجب	French fries	68	رقائق البطاطس المقلية
eye	22	عين	frog	12	ضفدع
eye glasses	45	نظارات	frost	94	جليد
eyebrow	22	حاجب	fruit juice	71	عصير فواكه

	English	Page	Arabic
	frying pan	29	مقلاة
	fuchsia	82	شجيرة الفوشية
G	galaxy	99	المجرة
	garage	81	مرآب
	garden	88	حديقة
	gardenia	83	شجرة الغاردينيا
	garlic	58	ثوم
	gas cap	72	غطاء خزان الوقود
	gas lighter	47	ولاعة غاز
	gas pump	81	مضخة وقود
	gas station	81	محطة وقود
	geranium	83	زهرة إبرة الراعي
	giraffe	17	زرافة
	glass	30	كأس
	globe	121	الكرة الأرضية
	glove	40	قفاز
	goat	9	ماعز
	golf	104	غولف
	goose	8	إوزة
	gorilla	17	غوريلا
	grape	56	عنب
	grapefruit	56	الكريفون
	grass	87	عشب
	grasshopper	10	جُندب
	gray	132	رمادي
	green	132	أخضر
	green bean	59	فاصوليا خضراء
	ground beef	65	لحم مفروم
	ground floor	24	الطابق الأرضي
	gull	5	نورس
H	hail	94	برَد
	hair	22	شعر
	hair dryer	45	مجفف شعر
	hairbrush	45	فرشاة شعر
	hairpin	45	دبوس شعر
	half past one	114	الساعة الواحدة والنصف
	hammer	49	مطرقة
	hand	21	يد
	hand gliding	103	طائرة شراعية
	handball	104	كرة اليد
	handlebars	75	مقود الدراجة
	handsaw	51	منشار يدوي
	harmonica	110	هارمونيكا
	harp	110	قيثارة
	harvest	88	حصاد
	hat	40	قبعة
	hawk	5	صقر
	hay	88	قش
	hazelnut	64	بندق
	head	21	رأس
	headlight	72	مصباح السيارة الأمامي
	hedgehog	20	قنفذ
	heel	23	كعب
	heel	41	كعب الحذاء
	helicopter	76	طائرة مروحية
	hemisphere	130	نصف كرة
	hen	8	دجاجة
	heron	5	مالك الحزين
	hexagon	131	مسدس
	high jump	104	الوثب العالي
	highway	80	طريق سريع
	hill	91	هضبة
	hip	23	وَرك
	hippopotamus	19	فرَس النهر
	hole puncher	123	مكبس ثقب الورق
	honey	97	عسل
	hood	72	غطاء المحرك
	hoof	9	حافر الفرس
	horn	19	قرن
	horse	9	حصان
	horse racing	104	سباق الأحصنة
	horse riding	104	ركوب الخيل
	hose	51	خرطوم مياه
	hour hand	114	عقرب الساعات
	house	24	بيت
	hurdles	104	سباق الحواجز
	hyacinth	83	زهرة الياقوتية
I	ice cream	69	المثلجات
	ice cube	71	مكعبات الثلج
	ice hockey	106	الهوكي على الجليد
	icicle	94	كتلة ثلج مدلاة
	iguana	12	إيغوانا
	index finger	23	السبابة
	ink	31	حبر
	iris	83	زهرة القزحية
	iron	37	مكواة
	ironing board	33	طاولة الكي
	island	89	جزيرة
J	jar	30	جرّة
	jasmine	83	ياسمين
	javelin	105	رياضة رمي الرمح
	jeans	39	سروال الجينز
	jellyfish	14	قنديل البحر
	jerrycan	33	وعاء لحمل الوقود
	jet ski	79	جت سكي
	jewellery	42	مجوهرات
	jonquil	83	النرجس الأسَلي
	judo	103	الجودو
	jug	30	إبريق
	juice extractor	31	عصّارة فواكه
	jumpsuit	38	بذلة
	jungle	92	أدغال
	Jupiter	98	كوكب المشتري
K	kangaroo	18	الكنغر
	key	47	مفتاح
	keyboard	52	لوحة المفاتيح
	kitchen	29	مطبخ
	kite	131	طائرة ورقية
	kitten	7	هرة صغيرة
	kiwi	56	كيوي
	knee	21	ركبة
	knife	30	سكين
	koala	16	الكوال
L	ladder	50	سلم
	ladybird	11	دعسوقة
	lake	90	بركة
	lamb	9	خروف
	lamp	34	مصباح
	lavender	83	الخزامى
	layer	91	طبقة

Index مؤشر

leaf	87	ورقة نبات
leek	61	الكُرّاث
leg	21	رجل
lemon	58	لَيمون
lemonade	71	عصير الليمون
lentils	66	عدس
leopard	18	فهد
lesson	118	درس
letters	122	رسائل
lettuce	61	خس
library	118	مكتبة
lightning	95	برق
lilac	84	زهر الليلك
lion	18	أسد
lip	22	شَفَة
little finger	23	خنصر
living room	25	غرفة الجلوس
lizard	12	سحلية
llama	18	حيوان اللاما
lobster	14	سرطان البحر
log	88	رند الخشب
long-nose pliers	48	كماشة طويلة الأنف
lovebird	5	طيور الحب
M magnet	120	مغناطيس
magnifying glass	120	عدسة مكبَّرة
magnolia	84	الماغنوليا
mallet	49	مطرقة خشبية
mandarin	56	ثمر اليوسفي
mandolin	110	آلة المندولين
mane	18	العُرف
mango	57	المانجو
manicure set	46	أدوات تقليم الأظافر
marathon	105	سباق المسافات الطويلة
market	54	سوق
marrow	60	قرع
Mars	98	المريخ
marsh	90	مستنقع
matchbox	47	علبة ثقاب
matchsticks	47	أعواد ثقاب
melon	56	شمّام
Mercury	98	كوكب عطارد
metronome	113	بندول الإيقاع
microphone	53	ميكروفون
microscope	121	مجهر
microwave oven	35	المايكرويف
middle finger	23	الإصبع الوسطى
midnight	117	منتصف الليل
milk	70	حليب
Milky Way	99	درب التبانة
millennium	115	ألفية
minivan	73	حافلة صغيرة
mint	61	نعناع
minus sign	135	إشارة الطرح
minute hand	114	عقرب الدقائق
mirror	27	مرآة
mole	20	خلد
mole wrench	48	مفتاح ربط
monitor	52	شاشة كومبيوتر
monkey	17	قرد
month	115	شهر
Moon	98	القمر
mop	33	ممسحة
mosquito	11	بَعوضة
moss	84	طحالب
moth	10	عُثّة
motorcycle	75	دراجة نارية
mountain	91	جبل
mountaineering	105	رياضة تسلّق الجبال
mouse	20	فأر
mouth	22	فم
mud	100	طين
multiplication sign	135	إشارة الضرب
museum	109	متحف
mushroom	58	فطر
music stand	113	حامل للنوتة الموسيقية
N nail	49	مسمار
nail clippers	46	قلامة أظافر
nail file	46	مبرد الأظافر
narcissus	84	زهر النرجس
navel	23	السُرة
neck	22	رقبة
necklace	42	عقد
Neptune	98	كَوكب نيبتون
nest	5	عش
nettle	84	نبات القُرّاص
newspaper	53	جريدة
newt	12	سمندل الماء
night	117	ليل
nine	126	تسعة
nineteen	127	تسعة عشر
nineteenth	127	التاسع عشر
ninety	129	تسعون
ninety-one	129	واحد وتسعون
ninth	125	التاسع
North America	96	أميريكا الشمالية
nose	22	أنف
notebook	119	مفكرة
nut	48	حزقة
O oats	86	الشوفان
oboe	111	مزمار
ocean	89	محيط
octagon	131	مثمَّن
octopus	14	أخطبوط
oil	67	زيت
okra	59	بامية
olive	67	زيتون
olive oil	67	زيت زيتون
one	124	واحد
one hundred	124	مئة
one hundred thousand	124	مئة ألف
one million	124	مليون
one o'clock	114	الساعة الواحدة
one thousand	124	ألف
onion	59	بصل
open ended wrench	48	مفتاح ذو نهايات مفتوحة
orange	56	برتقال
orange juice	71	عصير البرتقال
orchestra	109	أوركسترا
orchid	85	الأوركيد
ostrich	5	نعامة

otter	20	قُضاعة / كلب الماء
oven	35	فرن
owl	5	بومة
P_padlock	50	قفل
page	119	صفحة
palette	108	لوح ألوان الرسام
palm	21	كف
palm tree	86	شجرة نخيل
pancakes	63	فطائر
panda	19	الباندا
paper-clip	121	مشبك أوراق
parentheses	134	قوسان بين الكلام
parrot	5	ببغاء
parsley	61	بقدونس
passenger terminal	80	قاعة الركاب
passport	43	جواز سفر
pasta	66	معكرونة
path	92	ممر
peach	56	درّاق
peacock	5	طاووس
peanut	64	الفول السوداني
pear	57	إجاص / كمّثرى
peas	59	بازلاء
pebbles	90	حصاة
pedal	75	دواسة
pelican	6	طائر البجع
pen	119	قلم حبر
pencil	119	قلم رصاص
pencil sharpener	119	المبراة
penguin	15	البطريق
pentagon	131	المخمّس
pepper	58	فلفل
percent	135	في المئة
perfume	45	عطر
period	134	نقطة
pet	9	حيوان أليف
petal	87	نبات البتلة
piano	110	بيانو
pickax	51	معول
pickup truck	73	شاحنة
picture	108	لوحة
picture frame	108	إطار صورة
pie	63	فطيرة
pier	81	رصيف ممتد في البحر
pig	9	خنزير
pigeon	6	حمامة
pillow	26	وسادة
pine cone	86	كوز الصنوبر
pineapple	57	أناناس
pink	133	زهري
pins	47	دبابيس
pistachio	64	فستق حلبي
pizza	63	بيتزا
plate	30	طبق
playground	118	ملعب
plug	50	قابس كهرباء
plum	57	خوخ
plumbing	27	أنابيب المياه
plus sign	135	إشارة الجمع
pocket	38	جيب
polar bear	16	دب قطبي
police car	74	سيارة شرطة
pomegranate	57	رمّان
popcorn	69	الفشار
poppy	84	زهرة الخشخاش
port	81	ميناء
pot	29	إناء
potato	59	بطاطا
pressure cooker	29	قدر الضغط
printer	52	طابعة
puddle	100	بركة ماء صغيرة
pumpkin	59	قرع / يقطين
puppy	7	جرو
purple	133	أرجواني
purse	43	محفظة
pushpin	121	دبوس تثبيت
pyramid	131	هرم
Q_ quarter past one	114	الساعة الواحدة والربع
quarter to two	114	الساعة الثانية إلا ربع
question mark	135	إشارة استفهام
quince	57	سفرجل
quotation marks	134	علامات الاقتباس
R_ rabbit	20	أرنب
raccoon	16	حيوان الراكون
race car	74	سيارة سباق
radiator	34	جهاز تدفئة جداري
radio	53	راديو
radish	61	فجل
rafting	105	رياضة التجذيف الجماعي
railroad station	81	محطة قطار
railroad track	81	سكة قطار
rain	95	مطر
rake	51	مجرف
raspberry	55	توت
rat	20	جرذ
razor	46	شفرة
rectangle	130	مستطيل
red	133	أحمر
reel	44	بكرة خيطان
refrigerator	29	ثلاجة
restaurant	54	مطعم
rhinoceros	19	وحيد القرن
ribbon	44	شريط
rice	66	أرزّ
ring	42	خاتم
ring finger	23	إصبع البنصر
river	90	نهر
road	80	طريق
robin	4	طائر أبو الحن
rock	93	صخرة
rocking chair	25	كرسي هزاز
rocky landscape	93	مشهد طبيعة صخرية
rollerblade	75	حذاء تزلج
roof	24	سطح
room	25	غرفة
rooster	8	ديك
root	87	جذر
rope	51	حبل
rose	85	وردة
row boat	79	قارب تجذيف

rowing	105	تجذيف	shoulder bag	43	حقيبة كتف
rubber stamp	123	ختم	shovel	51	مجرفة
ruby	42	ياقوت	shower	27	دُش
rug	26	بساط	sidewalk	80	رصيف
ruler	120	مسطرة	single quotation marks	134	علامات اقتباس مفردة
rye	86	الجاودار	sink	31	حوض
S sack	33	كيس	six	125	ستة
saddle	75	مقعد دراجة	sixteen	127	ستة عشر
safety helmet	50	خوذة	sixteenth	127	السادس عشر
safety pin	47	دبوس أمان	sixth	125	السادس
sail	79	شراع	sixty	129	ستون
sailboat	79	قارب شراعي	sixty-one	129	واحد وستون
sailing	105	الإبحار	skeleton	22	هيكل عظمي
salad	68	سلطة	skiing	106	تزلج
salamander	13	السمندر	skirt	39	تنورة
salt	68	ملح	skull	22	جمجمة
sand	89	رمال	skunk	17	حيوان الظربان
sandal	41	صندل	sled	75	مزلجة
sandpit	118	حوض رمال	sleeping bag	107	كيس النوم
sandwich	63	سندويتش	slice of bread	62	شريحة من الخبز
satellite dish	99	طبق الأقمار الصناعية	slip joint pliers	48	كماشة ذو مفصل متحرّك
Saturn	98	كوكب زحل	slippers	41	خف
sausage	65	النقانق	slope	93	منحدر
saxophone	111	الساكسفون	snacks	68	وجبات خفيفة
scale	31	ميزان	snail	11	حلزون
scanner	52	جهاز الماسح الضوئي	snake	13	أفعة
scarf	40	وشاح	snapdragon	84	نبتة أنف العجل
scissors	120	مقص	snare drum	112	طبل ذو صوت حاد
scooter	75	دراجة بخارية صغيرة	sneakers	41	أحذية رياضية
scorpion	11	عقرب	snow	94	ثلج
screw	49	برغي	snowboarding	106	التزلج على الجليد
screwdriver	49	مفك البراغي	snowdrop	85	زهرة اللبن الثلجية
seahorse	15	فرس البحر	soap	27	صابون
seal	15	فقمة	soccer	106	كرة القدم
seaweed	15	عشب البحر	socks	41	جوارب
second	124	الثاني	sofa	25	أريكة
second hand	114	عقرب الثوان	soil	92	تربة
semicircle	130	نصف دائرة	soup	68	حساء
semicolon	134	فارزة منقوطة	South America	96	أميريكا الجنوبية
seven	125	سبعة	space	99	الفضاء
seventeen	127	سبعة عشر	space shuttle	99	مكوك فضائي
seventeenth	127	السابع عشر	space station	99	محطة فضائية
seventh	125	السابع	sparrow	6	عصفور الدوري
seventy	129	سبعون	speaker	53	مكبر الصوت
seventy-one	129	واحد وسبعون	speed skating	106	رياضة التزلج السريع
sewing machine	36	ماكينة خياطة	sphere	130	جسم كروي
sewing needle	47	إبرة خياطة	spider	11	عنكبوت
shaker	30	مذرّة	spinach	61	سبانخ
shark	15	سمك القرش	spirit level	48	ميزان تسوية
shaving brush	46	فرشاة حلاقة	spoke	72	مكبح
sheep	9	غنم	sponge	27	إسفنج
sheet	26	جوخ	spoon	30	ملعقة
shelf	27	رف	spring	116	فصل الربيع
shin	23	قصبة الرجل	spring onion	61	بصل أخضر
ship	78	سفينة	square	130	مربع
shirt	39	قميص	square root of	135	الجذر التربيعي
shoelaces	41	رباط الحذاء	squirrel	20	سنجاب
shoes	41	حذاء	stadium	106	مدرج الألعاب الرياضية
shorts	39	سروال قصير	stage	109	خشبة المسرح
shoulder	23	كتف	stamp	122	طابع

staple remover	123	مزيل مشبك الورق	thirteenth	126	الثالث عشر
stapler	123	كباس الورق	thirty	128	ثلاثون
staples	123	مشبك ورق سلكي	thirty-one	128	واحد وثلاثون
star	131	نجمة	thread	44	خيط
starfish	15	نجم البحر	three	124	ثلاثة
statue	108	تمثال	throat	23	حنجرة
steak	65	شريحة لحم	thumb	23	إبهام اليد
steering wheel	72	مقود	tie	40	ربطة عنق
stem	87	ساق النبات	tiger	18	نمر
steps	24	درج	timpani	112	دفية
stone	91	حجر	tire	72	عجلة
stool	28	مقعد	toad	13	ضفدع
stopwatch	107	ساعة التوقيف	toast	62	خبز محمص
stork	6	اللقلق	toaster	35	آلة تحميص الخبز
strawberry	55	فراولة	toe	21	إصبع قدم
stream	90	جدول	toilet	27	مرحاض
street	80	شارع	toilet paper	27	ورق الحمام
streetcar	77	الترام	tomato	59	طماطم
stroller	75	عربة أطفال	toolbox	58	علبة أدوات
submarine	79	غواصة	toothbrush	46	فرشاة أسنان
sugar	69	سكر	toothpaste	46	معجون أسنان
suit	38	بدلة	torch	50	مصباح يدوي
suitcase	43	حقيبة سفر	tornado	95	إعصار
summer	116	فصل الصيف	tortoise	13	سلحفاة
Sun	98	الشمس	tow truck	73	شاحنة لسحب السيارات
sunflower	86	زهرة عباد الشمس	towel	27	منشفة
sunglasses	45	نظارات شمسية	tracksuit	38	بدلة رياضية
sunrise	117	الشروق	tractor	74	جرار
supermarket	54	سوبر ماركت	traffic	80	المرور
swallow	6	طائر السنونو	traffic light	75	إشارة مرور
swan	6	بجعة	train	77	قطار
sweater	39	سترة	transporter	73	شاحنة نقل
swimming	107	السباحة	tree	87	شجرة
swimming pool	107	حوض سباحة	triangle	131	مثلث
swimming trunks	38	سروال السباحة	trombone	111	المردده، آلة موسيقية
swimsuit	38	ثوب السباحة	trousers	39	بنطال
T _ T-shirt	39	قميص قصير الكمّين	truck	73	شاحنة
table tennis	106	لعبة تنس الطاولة	trumpet	111	بوق
tableware	28	أدوات المائدة	trunk	72	صندوق السيارة
tadpole	13	شرغوف	tuba	111	نوع من الأبواق
taekwondo	103	التايكوندو	tulip	85	زهرة التوليب
tail	20	ذيل	tuning fork	113	الشوكة الرنانة
tambourine	112	دف صغير	tunnel	81	نفق
tape dispenser	121	موزع الشريط اللاصق	turkey	8	ديك حبش
tape measure	50	شريط القياس	turnip	60	لفت
tea	71	شاي	turtle	15	سلحفاة
teapot	31	إبريق الشاي	tusk	16	ناب
teaspoon	31	ملعقة شاي	tweezers	46	ملقط شعر صغير
telephone	52	هاتف	twelfth	126	الثاني عشر
telescope	121	منظار	twelve	126	إثنا عشر
television	37	تلفاز	twentieth	128	العشرون
ten	126	عشرة	twenty	128	عشرون
ten thousand	126	عشرة آلاف	twenty-first	128	الواحد والعشرون
tennis	107	لعبة التنس	twenty-one	128	واحد وعشرون
tent	107	خيمة	two	124	إثنان
tenth	126	العاشر	two hundred	124	مئتان
theater	109	مسرح	**U** _ umbrella	43	مظلة
thigh	21	فخذ	underground	77	قطار الأنفاق
third	124	الثالث	Uranus	98	أورانس
thirteen	126	ثلاثة عشر	**V** _ vacuum cleaner	37	مكنسة كهربائية

Index مؤشر

English	Page	Arabic
valley	92	وادي
van	73	شاحنة صغيرة
vase	33	مزهرية
Venus	98	كوكب فينوس
video camera	53	كاميرا فيديو
vineyard	86	كرم
violin	113	كمان
volcano	93	بركان
volleyball	105	الكرة الطائرة
vulture	6	نسر
W_ wagon	77	عربة
waist	21	خصر
walking stick	43	عصا المشي
wall	24	حائط
wallet	43	محفظة
walnut	65	جوز
walrus	15	حصان البحر
wardrobe	26	خزانة الثياب
washing machine	37	غسالة
wasp	11	دبور
waste basket	123	سلة مهملات
watch	42	ساعة يد
water	71	ماء
water lily	85	زنبق الماء
water polo	107	كرة الماء
water skiing	106	تزلج على الماء
waterfall	100	شلال
watermelon	56	بطيخ
watermill	100	طاحونة مياه
wave	100	موجة
weed	84	عشبة ضارة
week	115	أسبوع
weightlifting	102	رفع أثقال
whale	14	حوت
wheat	86	قمح
wheel	75	عجلة
wheelbarrow	51	عربة يدوية
whistle	123	صافرة
white	133	أبيض
wind	95	رياح
window	24	نافذة
windscreen	72	الزجاج الأمامي
windscreen wipers	72	ماسحات الزجاج
wing	6	جناح الطائر
wing	76	جناح الطائرة
winter	116	فصل الشتاء
wolf	17	ذئب
wood	88	خشب
woodpecker	6	نقار الخشب
wrestling	103	مصارعة
wrist	23	معصم
writing pad	123	مسند للكتابة
Y_ yacht	78	يخت
year	115	سنة
yellow	132	أصفر
yogurt	70	لبن
yolk	66	صفار البيض
Z_ zebra	19	حمار الوحش
zero	129	صفر
zipper	44	سحّاب